# INTIMACY:

## ISSUES OF EMOTIONAL LIVING
## IN AN AGE OF STRESS
## FOR CLERGY AND RELIGIOUS

# INTIMACY:

## ISSUES OF EMOTIONAL LIVING
## IN AN AGE OF STRESS
## FOR CLERGY AND RELIGIOUS

### THE THIRD
### PSYCHOTHEOLOGICAL SYMPOSIUM

PHILOMENA AGUDO

JAMES P. MADDEN

BERNARD J. BUSH

THOMAS J. TYRRELL

VIRGINIA O'REILLY

AUDREY E. CAMPBELL-WRAY

Edited by Anna Polcino, M.D.

With a Foreword by Thomas A. Kane

## AFFIRMATION BOOKS
### WHITINSVILLE, MASSACHUSETTS

PUBLISHED WITH ECCLESIASTICAL PERMISSION

First Edition
© 1978 by House of Affirmation, Inc.

Printed by Mercantile Printing Company, Worcester, MA
United States of America

To

present and former residents

of the House of Affirmation

with love and gratitude

# CONTENTS

# FOREWORD

Adult living is difficult work. Intimacy, which is necessary to all maturity, is a difficult and demanding process. Intimacy calls us to step out of our roles and let significant others see us not as we would like to be, strong and generous, brave and confident, but as we really are, weak and needy, scared and vulnerable. Such revelation to a significant other is done in truth and honesty; such revelation of one's soul must be received with serious sensitivity, sacredness, reverence, and respect. Souls are for cherishing; nothing else will do!

To be a priest or a religious, to be in ministry in 1978, is a great privilege of service to one's fellow human beings. It calls for great risk, for a quality of life that compels the world to take notice, to "see how [we] Christians love one another." But wounded healers are we who have been called to witness in a special way to the message and mission of Christ.

Intimacy with another human being brings the Christian to a closer and emotionally richer relationship with the Lord. A new vision of the Church as Mystical Body emerges when we are affirmed persons who live affirming others because we are intimately in the presence of Jesus the Christ. Those of us who struggle to live a life of intimacy are encouraged in Paul's prayer to the Church at Ephesus that "He may live in your hearts through faith, and then planted in love and built on love, you will with all the saints have the strength to grasp the breadth and length, the height and the depth, until knowing the love of Christ, which is beyond all knowledge, you are filled with the utter fullness of God" (Eph. 3:17-19).

Intimacy frightens nonaffirmed persons who often try to escape its embrace by retreating to workaholism. Such persons are so busy "doing" that other persons become objects. Such persons work so hard for the apostolate in the name of the Good

9

Shepherd that if He were to walk into the room they would be too busy doing "holy work" to even see or recognize Him. Workaholics, apostolic or otherwise, seek affirmation where it cannot be found, and, as a result, their desire for intimacy becomes futile and despairing.

When we look at the lives of the saints, we see several men and women who grew in intimacy with the Lord because of the intimacy they had with other persons. "In other words," writes Josef Pieper in *About Love,* the best available book on affirmation, "what we need over and above sheer existence is to be loved by another person. That is an astonishing fact when we consider it closely: the fact of creation needs continuation and perfection by the creative power of human love!" (p. 48).

There are those who insist that celibates should be intimate with all people but with no one person in particular. It is impossible to be such! No one can be intimate in general without first experiencing the intimacy of friendship with one particular person. Celibacy is a result of love, not a precondition of love. Authentic celibacy demands that one love each human person humanly.

Once again it is with pride that I recommend the following essays by my colleagues, who make no arrogant claims to new discoveries of affirmation, but who in all simplicity invite the reader to pause and to reflect on life's pilgrimage, which the authors share with all of their brothers and sisters. Their essays are not meant to be definitive statements concerning intimacy; rather, these essays represent an honest sharing of both personal reflection and clinical expertise.

Thomas A. Kane, Ph.D., D.P.S.
Priest, Diocese of Worcester
International Executive Director
House of Affirmation

# PREFACE

This book, the third in a series concerning issues of emotional living in an age of stress for clergy and religious, contains essays on various facets of intimacy—intimacy with self, with another and/or others, and with God. Like the essays in *Coping* and *Loneliness,* the first two books in the series, these essays are adapted from addresses given at an annual psychotheological symposium sponsored by the House of Affirmation, International Therapeutic Center for Clergy and Religious. But whereas *Coping* and *Loneliness* were the proceedings of the first and second annual symposiums held near Boston, *Intimacy* is the proceedings of two one-day symposiums, one held at Aquinas Junior College in Newton, Massachusetts, on October 1, 1977 and one held at Presentation High School in San Francisco, California, on November 12, 1977. Because attendance and audience response were so gratifying at both the East and West Coast locations, the House of Affirmation's psychotheological symposium henceforth will be held each year first in Boston and then in San Francisco.

As in past years, the theme of the 1977 symposium was chosen because it was the topic requested by so many priests and religious who attended the previous year's symposium. The choice was most appropriate because, as renewal continues in priestly and religious life, the need for intimacy among celibates is ever more evident. Many priests and religious are lonely and alienated because they have no meaningful interpersonal relationships. Much of this lack of relationship can be attributed to a pre-Vatican II way of life whereby friendship, if not actually discouraged, was certainly not encouraged and intimacy was a state to be shared with Christ and not with other human persons. But in our post-Vatican II attempts to remedy our neglect of human intimacy, we must be careful not to err in the other extreme and forget the importance of intimacy with God. The Trinity is the model for all human intimacy. The Father, Son, and Holy Spirit form a union wherein each person remains autonomous and unique. If we are not intimate with God, we are less able to be intimate with other human persons, for the relationship between the two experiences of intimacy is direct and profound.

Learning to be intimate is a process of psychological and spiritual growth and development, a process of relationship with the "other" that requires self-disclosure. We ask ourselves how much we should disclose, to whom, and when. Our answers are influenced by our capacity to trust and be trusted.

Love of God ought to enhance our love relationships and human intimacies. If we exclude God from these intimacies, we can become destructive to ourselves and to others. If as sexual beings we love not only God but human persons, we become living witnesses, passionate beings, who are fully alive and joyous. Rev. William McNamara states in his book, *Mystical Passion*:

> . . . Married lovers are not sexual and passionate enough. And what's more, neither are celibate lovers, who should be at least as sexual and passionate as married people. There is no other way to be a really great lover. And if religious men and women are not great lovers, what hope is there for Christianity?
>
> I stake the future on the few humble and hearty lovers who seek God passionately in the marvelous, messy world of redeemed and related realities that lie in front of our noses. These lovers may not be legion, but there is a sufficient number to reveal a Christlike way for married men and women to have intimate friends and for celibates to have chaste relationships that are obviously and joyously forms of appropriate interactions between highly sexed persons. I have met just enough of such happy, wholesome personalities to make me suitably optimistic to presume that the progress of Teilhard de Chardin's noosphere and the emotional maturation of mankind are in the process of being accomplished with such rapidity that an increasingly greater number of men and women benefit from such relationships.                    [Pp. 3-4]

I have known many priests and religious men and women who were so unaffirmed that intimacy was never a part of their lives. Some experienced real intimacy for the first time during psychotherapy. This experience changed their outlooks on life. They went on to seek God passionately and to relate intimately to other human beings.

We at the House of Affirmation have ministered to many religious professionals who have suffered because of the lack of intimacy in their lives. It is our hope that the essays in this volume will help all priests and religious understand the meaning and value of intimacy in the lives of celibate persons.

Especially grateful for having had the opportunity to moderate both the Boston and San Francisco symposiums, I wish to thank all those persons who helped make these symposiums possible and so successful. Accolades are due to the speakers and to the House of Affirmation staff, residents, and former residents from centers in Whitinsville and Boston, Massachusetts, and Montara, California. Special appreciation must go to the Sisters of St. Joseph for making available for the third time their facilities at Aquinas Junior College and for helping with the overflow crowd and to the Sisters of the Presentation for letting us use their high school theater. The Sisters of the Presentation and the young women of the Social Club certainly contributed to the success of our first San Francisco symposium. Last but not least, I must thank the more than one thousand individuals who attended the symposium in Boston and the more than five hundred persons who were present in San Francisco. The fact that many others who planned to attend the Boston symposium were turned away for lack of space has convinced us at the House of Affirmation that programs such as ours are much needed and wanted by our fellow priests and religious.

Sr. Anna Polcino, S.C.M.M., M.D.
Founder and International Psychiatric Director
House of Affirmation

Sister Philomena Agudo, F.M.M., Ph.D., is a full-time psychotherapist at the House of Affirmation in Whitinsville, Massachusetts. A member of the Franciscan Missionaries of Mary,
Sister Agudo received her undergraduate and early graduate
education in her native country, the Phillipines, at Our Lady of
Loretto College and at Ateneo University. She received her doctorate in pastoral psychology and counseling from Boston
University. Before joining the staff of the House of Affirmation, she worked at Boston's South End Center for Alcoholism,
at Lemuel Shattuck Hospital with terminal cancer patients, and
at the Danielson Counseling Center, Boston University. Before
coming to the United States, she served as a missioner in Indo-
nesia and Singapore.

# INTIMACY WITH THE SELF VS. SELF-ALIENATION

## Philomena Agudo

Every relationship starts with the self, and an intimacy with the self must set the foundation for the establishment of any mature and satisfactory relationship. Yet in our preoccupation with others or, in particular, a significant other, we forget the basis of every relationship—the self. Why do we need to relate to the self? Why do we need to know it intimately? Why do we need to understand it, to appreciate it, and to love it?

### THE SELF

The self is the core of a person's being. It is the personality center. Through the self we become aware of our uniqueness, our identity, our worth. It is the self that enables us to perceive reality in a certain manner and to give it an interpretation. Our values and attitudes toward life are formulated and shaped by the self. Being the organizational center of the personality, the self regulates our behavior. Our capacity for happiness depends upon a realistic concept of the self.

The concept of self is developed earlier than the concept of others. Our families and the people around us greatly influence the development of our self-image, but as beings with freedom, we are able to choose to accept and appreciate our authentic self or to reject and hate it. Our relationships with God and our fellow beings will depend on this choice.

## THE SELF AND GROWTH

During our developmental years, in our effort to adjust to our families and our peers, we find two selves emerging: the "authentic" self and the "masked" self. We make a choice about which of the two will form the core of our personality. To choose our authentic self is to fully accept our humanness; to recognize, accept, and respect our feelings by dealing with them honestly; to be aware of our gifts, our talents, and our potential, which we appreciate and use to the fullest for our own good and for the good of others. When we choose our authentic self, we are aware of the reality of human limitations and are willing to learn from mistakes and failures rather than be crushed by them. Since suffering is an inevitable reality of human life, the authentic self accepts suffering and seeks to discover its meaning. Choosing the authentic self is synonymous with choosing growth because the authentic self has a deep appreciation and gratitude for life.

The masked self comes into being in our effort to gain acceptance. It is the product of deprivation of love and fear of rejection during our early years. The masks form in layers that suit different people and situations. When we choose our masked self, we become the slave of unreal expectations. To gain acceptance, we suppress or camouflage our feelings, making honesty with regard to feelings impossible. When we choose our masked self, we fail to recognize human limitations, and we experience an obsessive desire for power in order to be accepted by others. We fail to appreciate our gifts or potential because we are driven to aspire to an unattainable ideal. The masked self compulsively desires to present a "super" or "perfect" image. The masked self has difficulty accepting failure or mistakes, which it interprets as crushing boulders instead of stepping stones. Suffering becomes a threat to the masked self's survival because that self is incapable of discovering a meaning to life. The masked self is so preoccupied with being accepted and at the same time is so inhibited from fear of rejection that for it life becomes a perpetual agony. Since the masked self does not appreciate life, it does not facilitate growth; it breeds self-destruction and death.

Intimacy with the self requires acceptance of the authentic self. When an individual's development has been arrested, or fixated, his or her emotional growth is inhibited, resulting in what we call neurosis. Yet an individual can be helped to outgrow that particular fixation. Growth, however, is impossible in the absence of an honest acceptance of the reality of one's emotional fixation and immaturity. Growth requires the full acceptance of and intimacy with the authentic self. An individual must decide and desire to grow, as a result being willing to experience the pain of being in touch with his or her feelings. Adjustment to people and situations is always accompanied by emotional tension and anxiety and is therefore painful. Intimacy with ourself enables us to be fully conscious of such emotional tension and anxiety. Instead of being paralyzed by it, we recognize and use it as a growth experience. Self-intimacy enables us to make a "growth choice" rather than a "fear choice."[1]

## SELF-INTIMACY AND PERSONALITY INTEGRATION

Personality integration is a lifetime process in which the faculties of an individual's personality work together in a smooth, coordinated whole. To make personality integration possible, we must be in close touch with the self. The ability to *listen* to oneself is an important factor in attaining personality integration. Integration of personality involves the smooth harmonization of feelings, thoughts, and behavior. A consistent or integrated personality results only when our ideations, emotions, and actions are in harmony. When an individual's mind is

1. A. H. Maslow, *The Farther Reaches of Human Nature* (New York: Esalen Books, 1975), p. 45.

full of happy thoughts caused by a joyful situation, that individual senses joyful feelings and his or her behavior expresses joy through smiles or laughter. If an individual habitually tries to deny these feelings of joy by showing anger or fear expressed as inappropriate behavior, he or she is certainly manifesting "self-alienation," or inconsistency or disharmony of self.

Personality integration is manifested in one's total acceptance of what one really is. When we accept ourselves for what we are, we cease to hunger for power or the acceptance of others because our self-intimacy reinforces our inner sense of security. We are no longer preoccupied with being powerful or popular. We no longer fear criticism or contradiction because we accept the reality of human limitations. Integrated, we are no longer plagued with the desire to please others because simply being true to ourselves brings us lasting inner peace. We accept our feelings as part of the self. We appreciate and listen to them. Accepting our feelings enables us to choose appropriate behavior patterns that are beneficial to ourselves and to others. Personality integration enables us to enjoy life responsibly and to discover the particular meaning of our own particular lives. We are grateful for life because we deeply appreciate and love ourselves.

Just as intimacy with the self facilitates personality integration, self-alienation fosters split personality. Self-alienation is the tendency to ignore, deny, or misperceive one's being and inner experiences. When we are self-alienated, we are fearful or ashamed of what is happening within. We suppress and fail to recognize our feelings. Consequently, our behavior becomes inconsistent or irresponsible. We experience a pervading sense of self-hate, and feelings of inferiority and inadequacy prevent us from functioning normally at any task. We are persistently compelled to put on different masks in order to relate to others or adjust to certain situations. Self-alienated, we survive by deceit and are mercilessly haunted by guilt. Our cycle of self-hatred is continual. Abraham H. Maslow aptly describes the difference between the split personality and the integrated personality: "To the extent that we are split, our expressions and communications are split, partial, onesided. To the extent that we are integrated, whole, unified, spontaneous, and fully functioning, to that extent are our expressions and communications complete, unique and idiosyncratic, alive and creative rather than inhibited, conventionalized and artificial, honest rather than phony."[2]

## THE SELF AND INTERPERSONAL RELATIONSHIPS

The French philosopher Jean Guitton points to the symbiosis that exists between self-love and love of others: ". . . love of another is inseparable from self-love. . . . it is impossible not to recognize that love is always in some degree, self-love. . . ."[3] If one's concept of love is that of benevolence expressed in care and concern for the well-being of another, this love is possible only when one cares for one's self and is also concerned for one's own well-being. If love is communion with the other, this communion is possible only if one has the capacity to commune with one's self. Christ based the commandment to love one's neighbor on love of one's self.

Self-intimacy presupposes a responsible love of self. This love of self is not the narcissistic self-preoccupation that excludes others. Intimacy with the self means listening to one's self, one's feelings, one's intuition and insights. It also means listening to one's body, its needs, and what promotes its well-being. If we are habitually attentive to our own needs and if we gratify those needs in a responsible and acceptable manner, we sharpen our capacity to be sensitive to the needs of others. We are able to extend ourselves to constructively promote what is beneficial to others. Self-intimacy strengthens our self-esteem and self-respect, the presence of which enables us to esteem and respect

---

2. Ibid., p. 157.
3. Jean Guitton, *Human Love* (Chicago: Franciscan Herald Press, 1966), pp. 67, 126.

others. Only when we are intimate with ourselves are we able to develop insights, interpret situations more accurately, and decide to behave in a way that is personally and socially acceptable. Most of life's situations have to be faced by what we call common sense. Common sense is simply wisdom from within. Every person (barring brain damage) is gifted with this inner wisdom, but continual listening to the self is necessary to getting in touch with its wellspring.

The capacity to love is a very important element in interpersonal relationships. This capacity is developed from infancy. If one's capacity to love is well developed, one is not bothered about the question of whether one is lovable or not. One is able to love without imposing demands on others. The capacity to love and accept others is strengthened by self-intimacy. When we feel secure within, we are able to accept others as they are; we are able to accept with calm both love and hostility from others.

Alienation from self increases the need to be loved and accepted but decreases the capacity to love. Self-hatred erects a barrier to satisfactory relationships. When an individual hates himself or herself, he or she operates by means of pretense and deceit. Since these means cannot be hidden from the self, contempt for self increases. Self-contempt, self-alienation, and self-hatred are expressed in hostility toward others. Such hostility breeds so much anxiety and guilt that an individual finds it impossible to enjoy any relationship at all.

Another effect of self-alienation is rigidity—the refusal to change or adapt to changing situations. Our feelings may congeal to the point of being callous. We find sensitivity to others impossible, and we begin to rationalize irresponsible behavior. Karen Horney describes such a development: "The more the emotions are checked, the more likely it is that emphasis will be placed upon intelligence. The expectation then will be that everything can be solved by sheer power of reasoning, as if mere knowledge of one's own problems would be sufficient to cure them. Or as if reasoning alone could cure all the troubles of the world!"[4] Anger at oneself gives vent to hostility. It appears as general irritability, as irritation at the same faults in others that one hates in one's self.[5]

Self-alienation results in self-destructive behavior. Freud mentions "death-wish" as an instinct in every human being. I would rather call this instinct the self-destruction tendency. The self-alienated individual will exhibit this tendency. Guilt and anxiety lay beneath the masks of self-alienation. A self-alienated individual's pervasive sense of guilt serves only to enhance his or her contempt of self. The self-hate fosters unconscious punitive behavior. Overwork, accident-proneness, compulsive eating, and alcohol or drug addiction are examples of attempts not only to drown guilt but to punish the hated self. Suicide does not happen on a sudden impulse. It is an act that has been rehearsed during years of unconscious punitive behavior patterns.

## SELF-INTIMACY AND GOD

In the Old Testament there is an account about Elijah the prophet who went up the mountain to seek God (1 Kings 20:11-13). A strong wind came by, then a terrible earthquake, followed by fire. Elijah did not find God in any of these powerful forces of nature. Instead, the "tiny whispering sound," the voice from within, brought about the communication between God and Elijah. The self is our main means of communication with God. But more often than not, we tend to overlook the eternal worth of the self. Yet, as we peruse the Gospels, we are amazed at how Christ not only affirms but points to how that self in every person is loved and valued. "As for you, every hair of your head has been counted; so do not be afraid of anything. You are

4. Karen Horney, *The Collected Works of Karen Horney,* vol. 1 (New York: Norton & Company, 1964), p. 85.
5. Ibid., p. 120.

10 : 30-31

worth more than an entire flock of sparrows" (Mt. 2:30-31) is a concrete way of saying, "I care for you; you are worth my life." The self is a gift; it is considered thus by Christ. When considering the self as a gift, we begin to understand why Christ suffered and died to redeem it. If this gift of self is precious enough in the eyes of God to warrant a Redeemer, how should we perceive the self? If we consider the self as a gift, we cannot help but be grateful for life and appreciate the talents and potential that accompanies it. I am firmly convinced of the fact that God has endowed every person with unique and special gifts. Persons need only be intimate with themselves in order to discover these hidden gifts. One example is one of your country's greatest inventors—Thomas Edison. He was considered unteachable in elementary school. He was hopeless in algebra. Fortunately, his mother understood and supported him. But most of all, he listened to himself and believed in the ideas that emerged from within. Had Edison been a self-alienated personality, we would still be reading by candlelight. Works of art in music or literature were created because certain persons discovered and appreciated the gifts with which they were endowed. We discover and appreciate our gifts only when we are self-intimate.

The awareness of the gifts of life, potential, and talents cannot but result in a deep sense of gratitude to our Creator. Self-intimacy therefore makes us open to a more personal relationship with God. It makes us open to grace. The great playwright Eugene O'Neill understood what self-intimacy means in relation to God when he wrote in his play, *The Great God Brown,* the following terse sentences: "Man is born broken. He lives by mending. The grace of God is glue."[6]

Self-intimacy, however, confronts us with that most unpleasant reality—our sinfulness, our propensity to sin despite our holiest resolutions. Yet it is this very sinfulness that merited for us a Divine Savior. At Easter vigil I always look forward to the

6. Arthur and Barbara Gelb, *O'Neill* (New York: Harper and Row, 1962), p. xxi.

chanting of the "Exultet," which contains the passage, "O happy fault that brought us a Redeemer." I also wonder who wrote it, for he certainly did not despise himself for being a sinner. To accept the reality of our sinfulness is to accept our authentic self. But self-alienated individuals use sinfulness as a valid reason for self-hate and self-destructive behavior.

Self-intimacy enables us to accept our sinfulness and to trust in God's mercy, but self-alienation leads us to self-contempt and distrust of God. Self-intimacy facilitates a deep personal relationship with God and satisfying relationships with others; self-alienation keeps God at a distance and inhibits sincere relationships with others. While self-intimacy enables us to perceive the commandments as God's way of protecting us from behavior that is destructive to self and others, self-alienation makes us interpret the commandments as God's excuse for being tyrannical and punitive.

CONCLUSION

In conclusion, I would like to mention one of our greatest saints, St. Augustine, who manifested characteristics of self-intimacy. He may not have written a day-to-day journal of his life, but he did write down his sins. He had a contemporary, a monk by the name of Pelagius, who could not come to terms with the sinful nature of man. He advocated that holiness could be achieved by sheer human will, that he did not need God's grace. St. Augustine, on the other hand, accepting his sinfulness, advocated the reality of his need for God's grace, for God's mercy. His self-acceptance made him open to holiness. The following quotation reveals St. Augustine's concept of love in Christian friendship, a love that is rooted in self-intimacy: "Love and do what you will; if you hold your peace, of love hold your peace; if you cry out, of love cry out; if you correct, of love correct; if you spare, spare through love; let the root of love be within; from this root nothing can spring but what is good."[7]

1. Sr. Marie Aquinas McNamara, O.P., *Friends and Friendship for Saint Augustine* (New York: Society of St. Paul, 1964), p. 226.

Reverend James P. Madden, C.S.C., M.A., S.T.M., C.A.G.S., is director of the Boston office of the House of Affirmation. A member of the Congregation of Holy Cross and a provincial councilor who was ordained in 1955, Father Madden studied theology at Notre Dame University and Catholic University. He received master's degrees in clinical psychology and theology from Catholic University and a Certificate of Advanced Graduate Study from Yale University. He also studied clinical pastoral education at St. Raphael's Hospital, New Haven, Connecticut. For many years he served overseas as a missioner in Dacca, Bangladesh. Upon returning, he was counselor and associate professor at King's College, Wilkes-Barre, Pennsylvania. Father Madden is a member of the American Society of Group Psychotherapy and Psychodrama and of several other professional societies. As an educator and a psychotherapist, he has lectured many times across the United States and in the British Isles.

# MATURED LOVE AND SEXUALITY: TWO SEPARATE ENTITIES?

## James P. Madden

If we are to learn to love with our whole selves, we obviously cannot do so as neuter "souls." Instead, we must learn to love as sexual men and women, attempting to love other sexual persons in a fully human way. In order to love maturely, we must integrate our sexuality, a vital element in our total affective drive, into the service of love. Christian thinking has long suspected affectionate love because it might lead to sexual misconduct. But such misconduct is a risk inherent in the human situation, to be guarded against but not to be allowed to deter us from our life effort to learn to love. This chapter concerns our human need to recognize ourselves and others as sexual persons. It considers the role of the body in human relationships and examines human sexuality as a healthy and positive dimension of personality that has broad expression in each person's words and work.

Emotionally mature persons can gaze inward on themselves without fearing what they might see. Such persons are open to the totality of their human experiences. Without being defensive, they can apprehend and accept their humanity, flawed though it may be, without undue uneasiness. The daily experiences of emotionally adult persons do not overwhelm or frighten them because they understand themselves. Such self-understanding is the foundation upon which any integration and mature control of the self must be built. In fact, friendliness to ourselves as we are is a first sign of emotional growth. Without such a healthy love of self, we can never be ourselves or give ourselves to anyone else. Theologians of every age have emphasized that the sinner fails not by loving himself too much but by failing to love himself enough.

Thus I shudder when I reflect on the sacred maxim of the Christian: "Love your neighbor as you love yourself." I shudder because I am so keenly aware of the psychological and emotional violence we do to ourselves in the process of our human growth. The Lord did not say "more than yourself" or "less than yourself" but "as yourself." Yet many of us priests and religious are uncomfortable with ourselves and consequently uneasy with others. Many priests and religious cannot accept themselves for what they are or love themselves in the human condition.

## GOD'S PRECIOUS GIFT: THE HUMAN PERSON

What are human persons? We are basically imperfect, fallible, and growing organisms, naturally growing toward wholeness. We make mistakes; we experience a litany of assorted and often strong impulses. We can fall short, but we can also measure up. We can get enthused, but we also can be utterly bored. We have high ideals and wild ideas all at the same time.

We must realize that we are less than perfect specimens. In fact, our troubles begin multiplying when we ignore or forget this truism. Human maturity, the integration of all that we are, *begins* only when we accept and embrace fully our incarnation in the human family. To state the matter more concretely, human sexuality is a healthy and positive dimension of personality that has a broad expression in each person's words and work. Human sexuality flows through us and deeply reflects and expresses us. Sexuality is and always will be a part of us as long as we draw breath.

If we allow our affection—our sexuality—to assume its proper role in our living—and our loving—then we must think of ourselves not as creatures composed of body and soul, as if these are two separate entities, but we must think of ourselves as sexual human beings whose bodies are ourselves even though not our whole selves. We must understand the role of our bodies as the means by which we are able to be present to others as well as to act for others, as our primary instruments in loving and carrying out the works of love.

Such a positive attitude toward human sexuality is quite natural to many persons. But a good many others develop such an attitude only after an agonizing process of facing their real distrust of and dislike for their bodies. Often various cultural and religious influences present in our childhoods caused us to distrust sexuality, to think of our bodies as both separate from and lower than our souls. Under these influences, we began to believe that sexuality belonged only to the body, whose parts were to be ignored as much as possible, except for whatever efforts were needed to regulate their activity.

Of course, such an attitude is not authentically Christian at all. Scripture perceives humans not as being composed of two separate entities, body and soul, but rather as constituting a body/spirit whole. The word "spirit" as used in scripture does not mean "not having a body"; it means "alive," "vital," "vivacious." In Hebrew, as well as in Greek and Latin, the word "spirit" is derived from the root meaning "breath." Because a living creature's breath was what indicated that it was alive, breath was thought to constitute the true vitality of a living thing, its "spirit." God is "Spirit" because he is the supremely living One, the One who gives us a share in his living beyond the living possible to other creatures; that is, men and women are capable of transcending their own knowledge and love, of being united with God and others in love, through their human life.

When St. Paul contrasts "flesh" to "spirit," he is not describing an opposition between body and soul but the difference between the whole person in the human conditions of weakness, sinfulness, and self-centeredness wherein he or she lacks the vitality and ability to love and the whole person made truly alive and able to transcend himself or herself in love by the Spirit of God. This gift of vitality and ability to love and so be united to the very Source of all love is what I believe is meant by the term "state of grace." This gift is what I interpret as our "spiritual life," that is, cooperating in the work of the Spirit with our whole selves—learning to love, making mistakes, and thereby advancing in the Spirit while doing the works of love and while being total human persons.

Psychologists often refer to terms such as "body image" and "self-image." Our body image is a part of our total self-image that deeply influences it. For example, a man who loses his teeth or his hair, whose body image has been altered, may experience changes in his self-image. Or a person who loses a leg or an eye may experience a deep sense of injury to his or her whole personality because his or her body is no longer whole. On the other hand, positive changes in our body image can do wonders for our self-image. For example, a shave may restore a man's feeling of self-respect or a new hair style may boost a woman's morale. Whatever makes us feel more becoming enables us to become more "ourselves."

Indeed, the scriptural view of human nature corresponds to the psychological reality of human nature. Thus we are able to welcome any scientific discoveries concerning the interaction of spirit and body. For example, we hope to learn more about how a strong spirit can operate in spite of a defective body, how terminally ill patients often manifest a deeper zest than ever before to reach out and embrace life. We hope to understand why some people who are physically unattractive nevertheless seem beautiful because of the radiance of their personalities, their presence. I recall my privileged audience with Pope John XXIII, who was very fat, with very large ears. When I entered with many fellow missionaries, Pope John was sitting on a throne that seemed to have engulfed him. His short legs dangled even with a cushion underneath them. He looked at our huge group, many of whom were very lean and gaunt looking, and said: "To paraphrase my patron, John the Baptizer, it seems that all of you must increase and [as he patted his girth] I must think seriously of decreasing." Pope John's charm, wit, warmth, and total humanness won the hearts of each of us in attendance.

## OUR BODIES: VEHICLES OF COMMUNICATION

What we think about our bodies and how we live in and through our bodies are important to human communication because our bodies are the essential element in all our relationships, in all our loving and living. Persons communicate only to the extent that they are willing and able to use their bodies as vehicles of communication, as means by which to gesture, touch, speak, and express a total attitude, an attitude that conveys the message: "I am with you; I am for you. I am glad to be with you, and I am trying to give you something of myself and to receive whatever of yourself you may want to give me."

Because the body is our primary instrument in expressing love, we need to cultivate all the formal and informal arts of communication, including the art of conversation and the art of expressing warm affection. Most of us are far too inhibited in this latter regard. Hesitating to use a warm handclasp in greeting, to put a reassuring arm around an anxious shoulder, and to embrace a dear friend whom one has not seen for a long time stifles affection. If we are to restore affection to its rightful role in the Christian life, we must find ways and means of expressing it through our bodies. We must deepen our awareness of what interferes with and what facilitates real communication, not in order to manipulate people more skillfully but rather to establish the best conditions for interpersonal affection.

We can be physically present to people with whom we have no desire to communicate, either because they are passing strangers or because we dislike them and therefore erect barriers that militate against communication, that effect a war of silence such as that that periodically occurs in our rectories and convents. But we can also be physically present to those persons with whom we are united in love, with whom we are able to communicate in silence.

All our loving is sexual in the sense that we love as sexual human persons. But we love differently in every relationship. A father does not love his daughter in the same manner that he loves his son, and a mother loves her son in a different manner than she loves her daughter. A brother's affection for a brother is quite different from his affection for a sister and vice versa. Friendship between women is something quite different from friendship between men, and, obviously, men and women experience their friendships for one another differently. Our human sexuality provides the differences proper to these various relationships.

Human sexuality and spirituality are not enemies but friends. A development of one does not mean a denial of the other. Both flow forth from the innermost center of human life. Our goal as priests and religious is not to choose between them but to integrate them, to be both spiritual and sexual, holy and sensual, at one and the same time. As Christians, we believe in incarnational spirituality and that the future life will be an embodiment of this being. Living "in the spirit" and "in Christ" does not mean alienating ourselves from our own physicality, but it does mean reaffirming our total selves as human beings who are sexually alive. We manifest this affirmation primarily in the affective bonds of permanent human friendships that are examples of God's way of loving us. We find this affirmation in community, in ministry, and in prayer. Periodically we should reflect honestly on the friendships we now have or have had and on the friendships we do not have and would like to have. Our failures at friendship are as important as our successes because we learn most by our failures.

## FRIENDSHIP: AN ONGOING PROCESS

Affective relationships, although beautiful, are not easy and painless. We need to be alert to this possibility in order to support our hope, and we need to be aware of those friendships that have not worked out so that we are realistic in what we encourage. There is always tension in life; the possibility of a tension-free life is a myth. Tensions arise from friendship as we integrate it into the total thrust of our lives.

What are two of the tensions we feel as priests and religious? We feel the tension between a particular friendship and our larger community, and we feel the tension that arises from the sexual dimension of a friendship. These tensions should not make us fearful of friendship or make us run from it. They are natural frustrations that have to be faced. They are not realities from which we should run but realities through which we should grow. Being totally present and being totally alive to the present mean taking risks and making mistakes. They mean asking ourselves very practical, honest questions such as: Do I own up to the fact that my relationship with my friend, male or female, is becoming less in accord with my commitment as I or we resent sharing our friendship with others? Am I honest with myself when I begin to expect or demand certain responses? Am I honest with myself when my friendship causes loss of interest in prayer? Am I honest with myself when my commitment to the members of my religious community suffers because of my emotional involvement? Questions of this nature, painful yet responsible, nourish our growth and integration into human life and demand genuine communication and a mutual love of God.

I honestly believe that there is no friendship without a purifying suffering. The love of friendship is not easy, but it does help to make life worthwhile and to give it deeper meaning. Growth in love involves all that the emotional, intellectual, and spiritual life can provide. It is a mandate of us who have taken seriously the primary command "to love one another as our Lord loves

us.'' I find it very interesting that the Gospels do not speak so
often of persons sinning or doing evil. They speak rather of persons who are lost and who find themselves not through fruitless
searching but through opening themselves to God. This openness regularly occurs in the context of their relationship to their
neighbors, in their response to others in the whole range of
human need. The Spirit reaches us as we open ourselves as men
and women to others. When we are closed to others, we close
ourselves to the action of the Spirit, and we shut out the real
source of our life and all that is truly a part of our life.

Emotionally mature sexuality, for married or celibate persons, flows out of their fuller growth as persons in relationship
to other persons under the guidance of the Spirit. This relationship is the mystery of the resurrected life we lead. Only by fully
accepting this life can we insure that our manhood or womanhood emerges. Faith in our healthy relatedness to the world of
men and women makes us whole and wholesome.

Consequently, we cannot discuss sexualilty or emotional
maturity except in deeply human terms, for it is through our
humanity that the Spirit acts, and it is to a fullness of our
humanity that the Spirit leads us. We cannot and we must not
expect this fullness to come overnight because human growth is
slow, demanding, and painful. Yet life is for those who love,
and human relationship is the fullness of life in which we find
the fullness of emotional and sexual maturity. The fruits, the
products, of our human living are inner peace and inner joy.
This reality draws each of us toward the Eternal Life, Light, and
Truth—the Incarnate Lord our God.

Reverend Bernard J. Bush, S.J., M.A., S.T.M., is director of the House of Affirmation in Montara, California. A member of the California Province of the Society of Jesus who was ordained in 1965, Father Bush studied theology at Regis College, Willowdale, Ontario. He served as student chaplain at the University of San Francisco before assuming the post of spiritual director at the Jesuit theologate in Berkeley, California. From there he went to Boston State Hospital where he interned in pastoral theology. In 1974, he joined the staff of the House of Affirmation and opened its Boston office. Father Bush has written numerous articles concerning spirituality and social justice, most notably in *The Way*. He has been active in the directed retreat movement and has lectured on Ignatian spirituality, religious life, mental health, and social justice.

# I HAVE CALLED YOU BY NAME

## Bernard J. Bush

Intimacy is always a rich and marvelous subject for consideration. Yet what makes it particularly exciting is that it is being discussed by us, a group of persons who presumably have vowed ourselves away from intimacy—human intimacy that is. We are those members of the church on earth who, at least until recently, were supposed to have room in our hearts exclusively for intimacy with God without human interference. Such duality, the either/or splitting between human and divine love, has been institutionalized in the states of life of marriage and religious celibacy. We are all familiar with the theological, spiritual, and emotional problems that such rigid compartmentalizing of Christian life has brought in its wake. Yet the changes that are presently occurring in the Church in response to these problems are attended by other no less serious problems. Thus it is most timely for religious and clergy to be reflecting on intimacy.

Intimacy is a word that describes a particular quality of a relationship. It implies knowing another and being known by another in the profoundest available depths of our being. However, before a relationship can progress to the point at which it could be called intimate, a kind of readiness for and openness to intimacy must be present in each person. By readiness I mean something more than the natural human disposition to have a close friend. Intimacy as Erik Erikson describes it can occur only when previous stages of emotional growth have been successfully passed through. Thus a person's capacity to experience intimacy is a matter of developmental rather than of chronological age. The passage to adulthood and readiness for intimacy can occur at any chronological age after adolescence. Erikson defines such a passage: "Womanhood arrives when attrac-

35

tiveness and experience have succeeded in selecting what is to be admitted to the welcome of the inner space 'for keeps.' "[1]

Irene de Castillejo, a Jungian analyst, in her excellent book, *Knowing Woman,* considers some of the qualities of the mystery she calls meeting:

> Why is it then that we meet so seldom? The curious thing is that we spend our lives not meeting people. All day we mix with others, in the bus, in shops, at work or play; but it may be that not once in the course of days or weeks or months do we meet any one of these people in such a way that a vibration is set up between the two. Nothing happens. . . .
>
> . . . Frequently husbands and wives have the closest physical intimacy for years and yet have no real meeting. Each is wrapped away in an isolation of his own.
>
> For there to be a meeting, it seems as though a third, a something else, is always present. You may call it Love or the Holy Spirit. Jungians would say that it is the presence of the Self. If this "Other" is present, there cannot have failed to be a meeting. . . .
>
> Sometimes I wonder if it is wise to work directly at relationship. What matters is to be centered oneself, willing and ready, always ready for the moments or hours of meeting when they come. Then the relationship can be trusted to take care of itself.[2]

De Castillejo identifies three barriers to meeting:

> . . . The first is that we are often living on a different level of awareness from the other person. The second is that one of us at least is often playing a role, or is somehow possessed. And the third is that we fail to listen to each other. . . .
>
> . . . One of the main reasons why we so often fail to meet other people is that we are so seldom really there.
>
> To begin with we are so often identified with our roles in society, and no one can meet a role. I cannot meet a doctor, a civil servant, a hospital nurse, or a shop girl unless these throw off their disguise and look me in the eye—any more than I can meet an acted Hamlet, though I might conceivably meet a real one. Similarly to be met I must be myself.[3]

---

1. Erik Erikson, *Identity, Youth and Crisis* (New York: W. W. Norton, 1968), p. 283.

2. Irene Claremont de Castillejo, *Knowing Woman: A Feminine Psychology* (New York: Harper and Row, 1973), pp. 11-13.

3. Ibid., pp. 14, 19.

It follows that once the Spirit has chosen to dwell in the open space created between people who have met, relationship can then progress and grow into intimacy. The criteria for the presence of the Spirit are beautifully defined in St. Paul's first letter to the Corinthians: "Love is patient; love is kind. Love is not jealous, it does not put on airs, it is not snobbish. . . . love seeks not its own interests nor does it brood over injuries. There is no limit to love's forebearance, to its trust, its hope, its power to endure" (1 Cor. 13:4-7).

The intimacy that follows from meeting will be the process of knowing the other and allowing oneself to be known by the other on increasingly deep levels. Such intimacy cannot be rushed, for successive revelations must be born when they are ripe. Forced or self-conscious sharing can inhibit growth in intimacy. The persons learn to flow through one another's lives without fear at various levels at various times. When a block is encountered, it is generally felt as fear or threat, and the defensive walls come up. Such responses require prayerful patience and reverential waiting.

IDENTITY PRIOR TO INTIMACY

Jerry Greenwald observes in his book, *Creative Intimacy,* that a strong self-concept is the foundation absolutely required for any intimate relating to another.[4] I would like to pause on this point for a moment. It might seem as if the priorities should be the other way around, namely that one would develop a strong sense of self-identity only through the experience of intimacy. But, I reemphasize, intimacy is a stage of development. It is a special type of relating that requires that previous stages have been passed through successfully. The previous stages of growth are the relationships that produce the self-confidence and self-possession that make the stage of intimacy possible.

---

4. Jerry A. Greenwald, *Creative Intimacy* (New York: Simon and Shuster, 1975).

I would like to cite two authors on this point. First, in a truly great work, *About Love,* from a Thomistic philosophical point of view, Josef Pieper states:

> . . . This desire for existential fulfillment, acting in us by virtue of Creation, is really "self-love." It is the basic form of love, which all others are founded on and which makes all others possible. At the same time it is the form of love most familiar to us from our inner knowledge of ourselves. Let us first consider this fact carefully. Then, perhaps, we may understand somewhat better why the love with which we love ourselves can be the standard for all other kinds of love.[5]

This love of self is the bedrock of Christian anthropology because the roots of relationship are in human existence itself. St. Thomas states that friendship is the image and self-love is the original; we love our friends as we love ourselves. If we argue that we do not feel friendship toward ourselves, St. Thomas would agree:

> . . . We do not feel friendship for ourselves, but something greater than friendship. . . . Everyone is at one with himself; and this being one is more than becoming one *(unitas est potior unione).* Just as unity is closer to the source than union, so the love with which a person loves himself is the origin and the root of friendship. For the friendship that we have for others consists in this, that we behave toward them as we do toward ourselves.[6]

Second, from a developmental psychological framework, Erikson describes the problem of trying to enter an intimate relationship when the proper foundations for identity and strong self-love have not been built:

> That many of our patients break down at an age which is properly considered more preadult than postadolescent is explained by the fact that often only an attempt to engage in intimate fellowship and competition or in sexual intimacy fully reveals the latent weakness of identity.

---

5. Josef Pieper, *About Love* (Chicago: Franciscan Herald Press, 1974), p. 82.

6. Ibid., p. 83.

True "engagement" with others is the result and the test of firm self-delineation. As the young individual seeks at least tentative forms of playful intimacy in friendship and competition, in sex play and love, in argument and gossip, he is apt to experience a peculiar strain, as if such tentative engagement might turn into an interpersonal fusion amounting to a loss of identity and requiring, therefore, a tense inner reservation, a caution in commitment. Where a youth does not resolve such strain, he may isolate himself and enter, at best, only stereotyped and formalized interpersonal relations; or he may, in repeated hectic attempts and dismal failures, seek intimacy with the most improbable partners. For where an assured sense of identity is missing, even friendships and affairs become desperate attempts at delineating the fuzzy outlines of identity by mutual narcissistic mirroring: to fall in love then often means to fall into one's mirror. . . .

. . . fusion with another becomes identity loss. A sudden collapse of all capacity for mutuality threatens, and a desperate wish ensues to start all over again, with a (quasideliberate) regression to a stage of basic bewilderment and rage such as only the very small child experiences.[7]

Erikson defines the opposite of intimacy thus:

The counterpart of intimacy is *distantiation:* the readiness to repudiate, isolate, and, if necessary, destroy those forces and people whose essence seems dangerous to one's own. Thus, the lasting consequence of the need for distantiation is the readiness to fortify one's territory of intimacy and solidarity and to view all outsiders with a fanatic "overvaluation of small differences" between the familiar and the foreign.[8]

This definition squares perfectly with our metaphysical premises. When inner unity is lacking, union is impossible, and attempts at union produce feelings of fear, panic, and loss of identity. Relationships thus begun invariably come to grief, usually without either person knowing why. Several such experiences can produce a most profound conviction that one is simply and constitutionally incapable of sustaining deep friendships. We could almost call such a state a soul-destroying sense of isolation and loneliness.

---

7. Erikson, pp. 167-68.

8. Ibid., p. 136.

This condition is prevalent among religious professionals whose life style prohibited and thus prevented their developing the identity that must precede intimacy. Our strong religious training emphasized that personal identity was the same as role or function. For example, I am a priest and a Jesuit, and you are a sister or a brother. The criteria for our successful integration have been spelled out in rules, traditions, personal documents, and saintly hero and heroine models for imitation. It is not surprising that from such a base our relationships tended to be stereotypical, service-oriented, and functional. If any of us got involved in a personal relationship that was apart from religious function, that relationship was seen as a positive threat to vocation.

Too often in the past religious professionals have experienced self-identity and ecclesial role identity as the same thing. At the expense of human development, some church and religious structures have reinforced this mistaken notion. For example, we need only reflect on the peculiar costumes, rigid rules and requirements for community living, and highly structured, "spontaneous" recreation that we used to call "organized joy." These and all the other externals of our life style tended to produce persons who fit roles well but who knew little about their human identity, especially their sexual identity. Without question, the women in the church have suffered more directly from this experience than have the men. But even though the men in the church have been in a position of ascendancy and seeming autonomy and control, the suppression (some might justifiably say oppression) of the feminine in the church has resulted in a corresponding emotional and human impoverishment of the masculine in it.

Yet the church alone cannot be blamed. The church is conditioned in its customs and styles by the world in which it exists, and the feminine influence is as much absent in secular society as it is absent in the life of the church. In a book entitled *Woman's*

*Mysteries,* M. Esther Harding points out the harmful effect this one-sidedness has had on society (and, I would argue, on the church):

> In Western patriarchal society, during many centuries, man was concerned to be dominant and superior, while woman was relegated to a position of dependence and inferiority. Consequently the feminine principle has not been adequately recognized or valued in our culture. And even today when outer manifestations of this one-sidedness have undergone considerable change, the psychological effects persist, and both men and women suffer from a maiming of the psyche, which should be whole.[9]

Persons are able to relate intimately only to the extent that they have achieved self-identity, and true self-identity is impossible without wholeness. Because suppression of the feminine element in society and the church has precluded wholeness and thus militated against intimacy, a renaissance of the feminine influence is of the utmost social and religious importance, for such a renaissance could well foster meetings between real persons that will replace encounters between players of roles.

## INTIMACY LEADS TO DEEPER PERSONAL GROWTH

At any given time in a relationship, the level of meeting is determined by several factors that progressively become apparent as the focused light of the other shines in our being. I most truly see and know myself when I see my image reflected in the eyes of someone who loves me. Yet, as Rev. Martin D'Arcy states in *The Mind and Heart of Love,* truly loving devotion always presupposes that the self and its dignity are not really threatened because only then can the lover freely and unreservedly, without a backward glance, surrender himself.[10]

---

9. M. Esther Harding, *Woman's Mysteries* (New York: G. P. Putnam, 1971), p. 105.

10. Martin D'Arcy, *The Mind and Heart of Love* (London, 1945), pp. 323, 325.

N B -    When we relate intimately with another, we discover to what
degree we are open to being known through and through and to
what degree we are guarded and self-defensive. We become,
sometimes painfully, aware of the extent to which we are free to
face ourselves and to accept another in our lives and of the way
our lives may be dominated by fear at its depths. We may find
that feelings that we thought were safely tucked away in their appropriate niches suddenly surface into consciousness and have to
be dealt with. Feelings such as anger, sadness, jealousy, awakened sexuality, tension, and grief now have to be faced and
shared with another. Such sharing, although a means by which
to work the feelings through rather than to repress them, can be
quite risky because it involves ever deepening trust in the other,
trust that the other will accept us as we are. Our false expectations about the other will be shattered by the reality that the
other is truly "other" and is much more than the projections of
our own unconscious. Commandments and taboos from childhood, suspicions and distrusts that have been held and reinforced throughout our lives can come loose with startling sud-
denness. Cherished beliefs and convictions become subject to
reevaluations that can cause a profound sense of loss of moral,
spiritual, intellectual, and emotional bearings. At such times,
consultation with a wise and experienced third person can help
to restore direction. But new bearings, beliefs, and convictions
will inevitably grow from a synchronicity with the intimate
other, for I am no longer able to force my behavior patterns or
role expectations onto the other as if I were the only person concerned. Of course, I and the other with whom I am intimate
must each retain ultimate responsibility before God. Such individual responsibility can never be shared away. Yet, through
the experience of intimacy, our stylized, prohibitive, and almost
strictly private conscience is gradually replaced by a more social
and relational conscience. To quote Erikson: "As areas of adult
responsibility are gradually delineated, as the competitive en-

counter, the erotic bond, and merciless enmity are differentiated from each other, they eventually become subject to that *ethical sense* which is the mark of the adult and which takes over from the ideological conviction of adolescence and the moralism of childhood."[11]

## ADAM AND EVE: ARCHETYPES
## OF HUMAN EXPERIENCE

Thus far I have spoken of intimacy in a general way. I have described some of its qualities and what we can expect to happen once an intimate relationship, that is, one in which knowing and being known by another, is occurring. Now I would like to focus more particularly on intimacy between men and women. Of course, what follows also can be applied to intimacy between men or between women. For example, ponder St. Gregory of Nazianzen's remarkable description of his friendship with St. Basil: "It seemed as though there were but one soul between us, having two bodies, and if we must not believe those who say that all things are in all things, yet you must believe this, that we were both in each one of us, and the one in the other."[12]

Yet, if we are to speak realistically of the challenge of intimacy for us today, I believe that the discussion should be directed toward celibate man-woman relationships. The subject is as vast and as varied as there are people relating to one another. Each person is at a different stage of development and of self-possession. With this fact in mind, I would like to recall the story of Adam and Eve from the book of Genesis.

I believe that in the heart of every man lingers what I call a 'suspicion of Eve'. From a man's point of view, Eve is presented

---

11. Erikson, p. 136.

12. Francis de Sales, *Introduction to the Devout Life,* quoted in William Johnston, *Silent Music* (New York: Harper and Row, 1974), p. 144.

in Genesis as the primal temptress. If you remember, Adam scapegoated Eve and accused her before God of having misled him. In Adam's case, what appeared at first as another's offer of a gift given in love and desire to share what the other perceived as good turned sour and resulted in personal trouble and anguish. I am sure that after the banishment from paradise, Adam continued to be suspicious of Eve's offerings. My point is that Adam (man) has never completely trusted Eve (woman) again, to this very day. A man's suspicion of the Eve in women, of the seducing temptress, causes him to hold back partly in fear of reprisals and unpleasant consequences, partly in anger to punish women for what Eve did, and partly from a pride that he can reconstruct the Eden he lost by his own unaided efforts. God announced that this tension and conflict between men and women would be the case when he said: "Yet your urge shall be for your husband, and he shall be your master" (Gen. 3:16).

This interpretation of scripture has been a strong theme in the writings of church theologians, exclusively male, who are perhaps converting their archetypal resentment toward women into theological dicta. The story of Adam and Eve, is, of course, a very sophisticated prophetic and theological reflection on the existing situation of men and women in relation to each other and to God. The myth arises from the collective unconscious of the human race, and thus it has universal appeal. The story of creation and The Fall elicits in us very powerful archetypal images that stir us and resonate at great depth when we ponder them. Because these images have the power to release our unconscious, we must be extremely careful about the way in which we interpret the images symbolically and act on them.

I believe that, placed in the context of the relationship of masculine to feminine and of humanity's relationship to God, the story of Adam and Eve is not intended to be either a general warning or a particular warning to the males of the species not to trust the females or vice versa. The story should not support the male belief that women are temptresses leading men from the path of virtue. Instead, the story is a statement of how things are and of God's belief that this reality is right and good. The story gives divine sanction to the tension between men and women as one of the elements in human history that prepares the way for the coming of the Savior, for only through the healing and reconciling presence of Christ and his Spirit of Love is the tension between men and women resolved and is humanity united. For example, recall de Castillejo's reference to the binding force, the mysterious third element, be it Love, the Holy Spirit, or the Self, that must be present if people are to truly meet. In this sense, meeting is a sacred event, an experience of reconciliation, however brief it might be. We might even say that in this sense meeting is an experience of the promised long-awaited coming of the Lord. St. Paul offers scriptural support: "If anyone is in Christ, he is a new creation. The old order has passed away; now all is new! All this has been done by God, who has reconciled us to himself through Christ and has given us the ministry of reconciliation" (2 Cor. 5:17) and "There does not exist among you Jew or Greek, slave or freeman, male or female. All are one in Christ Jesus" (Gal. 3:28).

What the story of Adam and Eve does not condone is divisiveness, blaming and accusing, or, as Erikson would say, *distantiation* between men and women. Yet these archetypal resentments exist, must be dealt with, and die slowly. In fact, they can be dissolved only if we men and women acknowledge their presence and invite the Spirit of the Redeemer to dwell in us as the healing and reconciling bond between us. Intimacy, then, is the process of offering and accepting mutual revelation in forgiveness and trust under the guidance of the Spirit. Or, stated in other words, intimacy is an expression of salvation through the reconciliation Christ came to effect.

## PERCEIVING THE SAME REALITY DIFFERENTLY

In a chapter entitled "Womanhood and the Inner Space" from *Identity, Youth and Crisis,* Erikson speaks convincingly of the different perceptual modalities of men and women. Basing his statements on controlled experiments and clinical observation, Erikson claims that women organize reality in terms of "inner space" while men structure knowledge around "outer space." He relates this practice to the basic physiological differences between women and men. Erikson then discusses how these differences of perception have affected the ways in which we humans try to discover God. He explains: "Man's Ultimate has too often been visualized as an infinity which begins where the male conquest of outer space ends, and a domain where an 'even more' omnipotent and omniscient Being must be submissively acknowledged. The Ultimate, however, may well be found to reside in the Immediate, which has so largely been the domain of woman and of the inward mind."[13] In the light of this observation, we can see that theology and the process of spiritual life, that is, growth in intimacy with God, must be a joint effort of men and women, an effort in which each sex's perceptions contribute to the fullness of human understanding and striving for God.

The concept and experience of intimacy as described from the male point of view tend to see the other as "out there" and to measure intimacy in geographical, spacial terms. Words like "closeness," "communication," "sharing," or "distance" come to mind. The man's experience of intimacy involves doing for the other, being supportive of another, expressing feelings of protectiveness toward the other, etc.

A woman's experience of intimacy is more likely to be expressed in terms of her own inner space, as holding within, including, incorporating the other into her being, welcoming and

---

13. Erikson, pp. 293-94.

assimilating the other, drinking in, being filled up, completed, rounded out by the other.

These differences of perception and inner feeling toward an experience that has the same name for both sexes, i.e., intimacy, can both enhance the relationship and produce incredible misunderstanding between people who are growing in intimacy. A man says, "Know me through what I do, what I produce, what I generate." A woman says, "Know me as I draw you within myself and show you inner treasures, as I offer you space to be yourself in my heart." Such offerings made with intensity of feeling can produce panic and fear in men and tears of frustration in women.

The perceptual differences can enhance relationships by illustrating the marvelous complementarity of the sexes. Neither mode of perception, either the masculine tendency toward outer reality and how man can control it or the feminine tendency with its inclusive interest in inner space, the relatedness of all things, and what fits or does not fit, is complete without the other. Men and women who seek to grow in intimacy must overcome hurdles. Both sexes must adjust to the sensitivities of the other. Women must come to understand that men are not being insensitive or uncaring when they express their outer-oriented concerns. Men must come to appreciate that they will not lose their identity or otherwise become swallowed up or emasculated by allowing themselves to be drawn into the center of a woman's life. Of course, both sexes must achieve considerable maturity before they are able to appreciate and be comfortable with their own perceptions and not become intolerably threatened by the constantly dawning awareness that there are different and quite valid perceptions of the same reality. Many relationships founder on the rocks of anxiety and inflexible defensiveness because the persons involved never reach such an understanding. Sometimes people who have progressed in a relationship to the point of being truly intimate suddenly panic and want out or feel that the bonds of unity they are experiencing must be expressed sexually or formalized by marriage.

On the contrary, Teilhard de Chardin envisioned intimate celibate friendships that would represent an advance in the evolutionary development of humanity. He stated in his well-known essay "The Evolution of Chastity": "Some day, after having tamed the ether, the winds, the seas, and gravity, we will capture, for God, the energies of love. And then for the second time in the history of the world, man will have discovered fire."[14]

## HUMAN INTIMACY RELATES TO DIVINE INTIMACY

I believe that there is an important correlation between the personal experience of an intimate human relationship and our relationship with God. Intimacy is being known and knowing. In the experience of being known by another and being accepted for who we are, we grow in the consciousness that it is wonderful that we exist. We come slowly to believe that the parts of ourselves that we find unacceptable, that we hate or are ashamed of or embarassed by, can in fact be accepted by someone else. We then learn to own and love every aspect of ourselves, our history, the gamut of our feelings, even our sinfulness. When we have been deeply affirmed by someone who really knows us, who has gotten behind all our facades and false fronts, we know that God loves us also, precisely because of the fact that he knows us and causes us to exist.

Thus there is a harmony between growth in human and divine intimacy and friendship. Elsewhere I have discussed the barriers

---

14. Teilhard de Chardin, "The Evolution of Chastity," as quoted in Rev. Richard W. Kropf, "The 'Third Way,'" *Sisters Today* 47 (January 1976), p. 271. For additional reflection on the thought of Teilhard and the influence women had on his thought and the development of his creativity, see William Johnston, "Mystical Friendship," in *Silent Music* (New York: Harper and Row, 1974), pp. 157ff.

we erect between ourselves and God.[15] I have spoken of how we often project our inmost feelings about ourselves and imagine that God feels the same about us as we do about ourselves. In this way, we create a false image of God. However, if we find in our relation to another person that the image of ourselves that we project is not the one that is reflected back, we must pause and question whether we know ourselves as well as we think. We have all had the experience of holding back in our relationships while thinking that if the other person really knew us, or knew such and so about us, he or she would not like us anymore or would even retreat in horror. As we grow in intimacy and trust and take the risk of revealing ourselves, we will most often find that the opposite is true. Usually, self-revelation and trust create the space and freedom for the other to reveal himself or herself honestly also. Such mutual sharing constitutes the process of growth in intimacy. It is a process grounded in knowing the other and being known by another in our deepest available places. Of course, all of what I have said presupposes a firm sense of identity, personal maturity, and vocational commitment. Only on such bedrock can the tower of mutual self-revelation be built. A relationship built on the sand of a shaky identity will be smashed by the storms that will inevitably come from the unconscious. A tower can be built only as strong or as high as its foundation is solid.

Scripture is full of examples of affirming intimacy. In fact, the whole of sacred scripture can be seen as the progressive unfolding of God's intentions and initiatives to establish bonds of intimacy between himself and humanity. For example, the prodigal son was projecting his self-image onto his father. He was full of remorse, guilt, shame, and self-abasement. His father knew him better and reflected quite a different image. It was one

15. Bernard J. Bush, "Coping with God," in *Coping: Issues of Emotional Living in an Age of Stress for Clergy and Religious* (Whitinsville, MA: Affirmation Books, 1976), pp. 71-83.

of compassion, understanding, tender forgiveness, and, above all, joy. The son risked self-revelation and invited punishment or even rejection. What he got was total acceptance. The sculpture of the prodigal son in the courtyard of the National Cathedral shows the father enfolding and including the son in a tender embrace. The story and the sculpture accurately depict the feminine side of God's nature. The gesture is not the more typically masculine response of sitting the son down to have a heart to heart talk, of saying, "Now son, what have you learned from all this?" On the contrary, the gesture is a joyful, tearful embrace.

In many instances we see Jesus, who is the absolutely perfect projection of the image of God, showing us God's true feelings toward us. The people Jesus meets in scripture are in fact you and I. The way he relates to them is how he relates to us. The intimacy he offers them, he offers us also. I am not just speaking of a Jesus out there, very distant and historical, but of the Jesus in each one of us. The miracle of our faith is that the bond between us is truly the Holy Spirit of God, his Love incarnate in each of us. To the extent that we are each in the possession of God's love, we can depend on acceptance from one another. "See how these Christians love one another?" We are called to intimacy just as the disciples were called even though they sometimes felt the fear of it and cried out, "Depart from me for I am a sinful man" (Luke 5:8). The scriptural examples of Jesus' close relationships with a variety of persons, in fact with whoever was open to it, command us to go and do likewise. The bond between us is love, and where there is love, the obstacles to union and a life of intimate sharing melt in the fire.

If we hold back because of fear or panic or self-protective defensiveness, we will become isolated, lonely, sterile. In this instance, the usual method of escape from self is to become busy with good works. How many of us settle for approval or attention because we fear affection? How many of us point to our accomplishments in the name of God's holy service as a substitute for letting anyone get close to us? Yet how lonely many of us are ultimately. Still it is much easier to share our works with others than to share our very lives. It is much easier to stake our reputations on the successful accomplishment of jobs than to entrust ourselves into the hands of another. But Christ said, "I call you friends, not slaves" (John 15:15).

## THE NAME BY WHICH GOD KNOWS US

I sometimes use the following exercise in imagination with my clients. Imagine that God walks in the door, comes right up to you, looks you squarely in the eye, and calls you by one word. What is that word? What is the word that God knows you by, that is the entire sum of God's knowledge of you and relation to you? It will be an intimate word. It will define your whole being. Is it a condemnatory word, a judging word, a congratulatory word, or a word of affection?

Now imagine that the person who loves you and knows you better than anyone else in the world does the same thing. This person is known by you for the constancy of his or her relation to you. Through thick and thin, he or she has stuck by you. You know of his or her faithfulness, which has been often tested. When that person says the word by which he or she knows you, what is it? Is it the same word by which God knows you?

I truly believe that growth in our humanity, as well as growth in our spirit, is the progressive discovery of the mystical name by which God knows us. It is the name written on the white stone, the name that only God knows. "To the victor will I give the hidden mannah; I will also give him a white stone upon which is inscribed a new name, to be known only by him who receives it" (Rev. 2:17). I am sure that we have all heard the name during our lives. We have heard it especially from those with whom we have been intimate. The tone and accent with which the word is spoken is more important than the word itself. After all, God calls Israel "maggot" and "worm" in Isaiah (41:14), and yet these epithets are heard as terms of endearment because they are spoken with love.

I do not think we are truly ourselves or are truly whole until we have heard that word from another human being. For most of us, deaf and full of preconceptions about ourselves, the word must be spoken repeatedly before we finally hear it. It penetrates only when we are absolutely convinced that it is being said by someone who knows us thoroughly. Only then does the word get through to the place wherein we define ourselves. It rings true through every fiber and reverberates with joy to everyone we meet. It even makes heaven happy because another person has finally heard and accepted the incredible gift that God has given us, that we should know and be known, love and be loved by one another. In short, we have become intimate. That word is the sweetest sound we will ever hear. That word is our very own name, spoken with infinite and eternal love. It is what Magdalene heard and responded to when Jesus in the garden said simply, "Mary."

In exchange, God has given us his own name so that we will know him also. Jesus has revealed the name of God to be Father, a father whose paternity extends to all who believe in his son. "To them I have revealed your name, and I will continue to reveal it so that your love for me may live in them" (John 17:26). This statement is the ultimate comment on human and divine intimacy, on living in one another and revealing our names to one another.

Thomas J. Tyrrell, Ph.D., is a full-time psychotherapist at the House of Affirmation in Whitinsville, Massachusetts. He received an undergraduate degree in psychology at the State University of New York at Oswego; a master's degree in school psychology at George Peabody College, Nashville, Tennessee; and a doctorate in clinical psychology at Duquesne University, Pittsburgh, Pennsylvania. In each of these programs, he minored in philosophy. He has taught the psychology of personality development at both the undergraduate and graduate levels, as an assistant professor at Constantin Liberal Arts College & Institute for Philosophic Studies, Irving, Texas, and as an assistant professor at Seton Hill College, Greensburg, Pennsylvania. He has had thirteen years of clinical experience in therapeutic psychology, personality assessment, and therapy supervision in various mental health and counseling programs. Dr. Tyrrell, a member of the American Psychological Association, Division of Philosophical Studies, and the Massachusetts Psychological Association, has lectured in the United States and Canada and is now engaged in writing a book on personality development.

# INTIMACY, SEXUALITY, and INFATUATION

## Thomas J. Tyrrell

Intimacy is a term used to describe the quality of many different types of interpersonal relationships, including, for example, relationships between sex partners, between close friends, and between parents and their children. Whatever the character of the relationship, the individuals concerned experience intimacy as a moment during which they find themselves being deeply and wholly touched by another. This moment can occur at any time—during an affectionate or a consoling embrace or simply during the exchange of a knowing glance. Thus the intimate experience of being deeply and wholly touched is not synonymous with tactility. Intimacy does not require being touched physically, but it also does not exclude or preclude it.

During a moment of intimacy, tactile or otherwise, we find ourselves deeply, often visibly, moved by a touch that has penetrated to the core of who we are as persons. We find ourselves opened up, exposed, made visible. At times the moment can be painful, and we suffer, but in the Latin (*sufferre*) sense of "to be open." What makes this moment so often painful is our egocentricity, a characteristic common to our culture, particularly our Western culture. As egocentrists, we tend to make demands of others. We demand that others know our hearts and that we be allowed to know their hearts. We want others to be God for us and to permit us to be God for them. We have great difficulty being ourselves and allowing other people to be themselves. We want to center our lives around other persons, and we often expect them to center their lives around us.

But such demands militate against intimacy, for deeply intimate moments occur only when relationships are authentic, autonomous, and free. Intimacy is a gift. No one can make it happen. If we set out to love certain persons, their love will elude us, for our pursuit of intimacy will preclude intimacy. Intimacy goes beyond the pursuit, the idealization of love, that idealization that we call infatuation. Intimacy goes beyond the natural narcissism of being in love. When we love persons, we tend always to want to dominate them, to take over, to control them. We want to decide what is best for them. Human love tends to be rather impulsive, rather controlling. Human love tends to stop at the bodily level. Thus we need terms such as affectivity, affection, and genital sex, terms that distinguish other experiences from intimacy. Intimate moments may include these experiences, but affectivity, affection, and genital sex do not themselves constitute intimacy.

So what is intimacy? Suffice it at this point to say that interpersonal intimacy is a moment of being wholly and deeply touched by another human being. This experience of being wholly and deeply touched is captured in Psalm 139:

I.

> O Lord, you have probed me and you know me;
>    you know when I sit and when I stand;
>    you understand my thoughts from afar.
> My journeys and my rest you scrutinize,
>  ˙ with all my ways you are familiar.
> Even before a word is on my tongue,
>    behold, O Lord, you know the whole of it.
> Behind me and before, you hem me in
>    and rest your hand upon me.
> Such knowledge is too wonderful for me;
>    too lofty for me to attain.

II.

> Where can I go from your spirit?
>    from your presence where can I flee?

If I go up to the heavens, you are there;
  if I sink to the nether world, you are present there.
If I take the wings of the dawn,
  if I settle at the farthest limits of the sea,
Even there your hand shall guide me,
  and your right hand hold me fast.
If I say, "Surely the darkness shall hide me,
  and night shall be my light"—
For you darkness itself is not dark
  and night shines as the day.

III.

Truly you have formed my inmost being;
  you knit me in my mother's womb.
I give you thanks that I am fearfully, wonderfully
  made; wonderful are your works.
My soul also you knew full well;
  nor was my frame unknown to you
When I was made in secret,
  when I was fashioned in the depths of the earth.
Your eyes have seen my actions;
  in your book they are all written;
  my days were limited before one of them existed.

[1-18]

IV.

. . . . . . . . . .

Probe me, O God, and know my heart;
  try me, and know my thoughts;
See if my way is crooked,
  and lead me in the way of old.

[23-24]

The structure of intimacy and all of its features that I wish to discuss are contained within this psalm. The psalmist acknowledges that the world is a fearful, wonderful, and fascinating place and that man and woman are fearfully and wonderfully made. The psalmist calls us to be intimate with the Lord, to go beyond the human, but he warns us that we must be human first, that we should not try to circumvent our humanity, that we reach the divine through the human. The psalmist is open to the fascinating, wonderful work of creation; he risks, surrenders, and willingly obeys. Such fascination, risk, surrender, and willing obedience are necessary to intimacy whereby we become our deepest selves.

## AN INVITATION TO CHASTEN OUR LIVES

Persons called to a life of celibacy must seek intimacy with God, of course, but they also must seek intimacy with other human persons. The psalmist tells us that we cannot become intimate by avoiding or repressing or denying the human, that we must remember our origins. We are all human beings conceived during a human act in which the sacred and the profane can be integrated. The psalmist tells us that the call to celibacy is a call to be human and is answered best by going deeper into life and not by going under, around, or above it. Celibate persons should celebrate, relish, and enjoy life. They should acknowledge that they are human beings whose origin is simultaneously divine and human. They should see the divine in the sexual act, the act of human creation, and acknowledge their sexual selves, their maleness or femaleness. No person can go deeper into life by denying the human.

We are awed that the notion of celibacy suggests that we become chaste. Yet chastity is not restricted to a life of celibacy; it is a call to all Christians, for chastity means becoming respectfully reverent to the whole of life. Thus all human beings are called to be chaste, to acknowledge the whole of life, and to integrate it. We are all called to go the route of love, and to go this route is to go the route of human experience. The psalmist tells us that we cannot just attach ourselves to the surface of life, that we cannot pretend not to be human.

## REPRESSION AS A DENIAL OF INTIMACY

But how can we plumb the depths of life? We can do so in one of three ways: solitude, another person, and the group. I have chosen to focus only on the second of these three ways, on the interpersonal, because it is here that the problem of intimacy surfaces vis-à-vis the psychologist. In therapy we psychologists time and time again meet people who are confused by intimacy, who try in their interpersonal lives to repress, avoid, and deny the need, the desire for human intimacy. These persons strive first for spiritual intimacy, forgetting that they are incarnate spirits. They try to lead an angelic life at the expense of the human. Such persons often either refuse or are unable to comfort one another because they cannot risk exposing their feelings; in fact, they have lost touch with their feelings. They do not have, or they have lost, that interpersonal skill that Alan Watts called the "art of feeling."[1]

Repressed persons, especially, refuse or are unable to be open, to be intimate. They try to stifle their feelings of affection, their care and concern, and, to an even greater degree, their sexual identities and feelings. Alan Watts says such persons are living out of their heads. Their thoughts, he says, come before their feelings. Such persons are intellectual porcupines whose surface is covered with spikes. Their every word, every action, warns others to stay away, not to get close, keep their distance. Such persons even take distance from themselves. Often they hide their bodies under layers of clothing that so cleverly disguise the fact that somebody is wearing them that you wonder if that somebody is a man or woman. These persons lead an isolated existence, cut off from others, as if they have no body.

Repressed persons fail to realize that by refusing or being unable to be open and available to others on a personal level,

---

1. Alan Watts, *Nature, Man and Woman* (New York: Vintage Books, 1970), Ch. 3.

that by refusing to express their feelings of care and concern, they have closed off an important avenue through which they could meet the Holy. Eventually, such persons are unable to be intimate not only with others but with themselves as well. Their moments of solitude soon regress into pietistic narcissism, at which point they have lost the possibility of being intimate and are unable to promote love of self and love of others. As a result, they become chronically depressed, chronically anxious.

In the course of therapy, we discover that such persons have confused what we call existential or personal intimacy with genital intimacy. Using St. Matthew as a literal guide in their interpersonal conduct, they have interpreted the meaning of intimacy to be merely sexual, and they make themselves eunuchs in the kingdom of heaven (Matt. 19:11-12). They fail to realize that St. Matthew was issuing a call to chasten and not deny our sexual selves. St. Matthew asks us to get detached from the pursuit of sexual pleasure. Neither St. Matthew nor St. Paul nor the spiritual doctors such as St. John of the Cross tells us to desexualize ourselves. They do not say that sexual feelings are evil. Quite the opposite, the canticle of St. John of the Cross is a very erotic poem. Scripture teaches that sexual feelings are a means to greater joy and are beautiful when practiced at the right time, in the right place, and with an attitude of reverence. After all, every interpersonal act is sexual. Think about this fact for a minute. I am not saying that these acts are genital, for they most often are not. They are sexual simply because being human is to be a sexed being, a being to whom the world reveals itself through a sexually differentiated body.[2]

Any human contact that intends intimacy is an unchaste act if it is impersonal. When we deny our sex, we cannot relate with our whole person because part of us is left out. Denying our femaleness or maleness will lead inevitably to impersonal con-

2. Maurice Merleau-Ponty, *The Phenomenology of Perception* (New York: Humanities Press, 1962), Pt. 1, Ch. 6.

tact because all of us are sexed persons. We reveal ourselves to each other through our male or female bodies. These bodies are intended to complement one another. Consider: does the human body make any sense if we do not think of it in terms of male and female in relation to each other? Actually, the human body is a rather weird looking instrument. In C. S. Lewis's book, *Out of the Silent Planet,* Professor Ransom has been living on Mars for a very long time. At one point he sees a couple of sausage-shaped creatures with a fringe of fur about their heads and faces waddling over the horizon. These creatures have peculiar elongated things attached to the top part of their structure, and they have peculiar flat things attached to long sticks on the bottom. In a moment of awareness, Ransom discovers that he has observed men from a Martian perspective, and he realizes what strange, clumsy creatures we are.[3] Other creatures are much more graceful than we, and yet we are fearfully, wonderfully made, made in relation to each other.

Repressed persons have separated sexuality from the whole of their lives; they have carved it out of the whole of their existence. In so doing, they have allowed sexuality to assume a power it does not ordinarily have or warrant; they have made sex an object to be idolized. They then must labor to keep sex isolated. But the more they labor, the more powerful genital sex becomes and the more they as sexually repressed persons become idolators. They encounter other persons not as persons but as objects to be either avoided or feared. Their anxious preoccupation with the isolated genital sexual act destroys their ability to freely, openly, and richly encounter anyone, most especially the opposite sex. By denying their bodies and their feelings, they deny intimacy with others. By carving sexuality out of their lives, repressed persons deny the mystery that is revealed by sexual differences. For them the work of creation has ceased to be a

---

3. C. S. Lewis, *Out of the Silent Planet* (New York: Macmillan, 1965).

wonderful work of the Holy and has become instead a problem to be avoided. They must avoid interpersonal contact, especially when they must express feelings toward others, for their feelings toward others, especially the sexual ones, are dangerous.

## INTEGRATION AND INTERPERSONAL INTIMACY

When we are in the presence of others, we find ourselves awakening, that is, if we are the least little bit alive to ourselves. We are awakened by the dynamism of intimacy. Intimacy is a call that we hear whenever two of us gather together. Persons who deny their sexual awareness must refuse to acknowledge this call; they must refuse to acknowledge their needs, wants, and desires. They are not able to be open to the beauty of the interpersonal because they must avoid the interpersonal. They therefore never experience moments of being wholly and deeply touched by others. Having become stale, dry, and dead, the interpersonal no longer attracts them. The wonder and mystery of personal intimacy cannot call them because its voice has been stilled. But the sexual detachment of the repressed person should never be mistaken as spiritual detachment, at least not the kind that is called for by John of the Cross. Repressed persons can no longer be interpersonally holy because, having denied their bodies and feelings, they have isolated their sacred and their profane being in the interpersonal world. Persons who have separated the spiritual and the profane, who deny that they have bodies, have withdrawn from the interpersonal world.

By means of bodies, we are able to become present and accessible to each other; but repressed persons have become absent, distracted, inaccessible. They can no longer play. When we deny our feelings, play and celebration become occasions for work. Repressed persons are notorious liturgical laborers; they *are* workers for the Lord, but they are *just* workers. They cannot celebrate the Lord's presence.

## NEED FOR A PERSONAL RESPONSE

By denying their feelings and their bodies, repressed persons deny their own histories, for it is through the body that both the past and the present live. When we deny our feelings, we deny the here and now, and reality is then displaced by voices from the painful past. Because in the past intimacy has always been accompanied by pain we repress and avoid it in an effort to avoid pain; but by so doing we avoid life. Our bodies orient us to time, place, and person; by denying our bodies we become no where, no place, no body. It is therefore not surprising that repressed persons are confused. They have no personal identity; so they must cling to their offices, sometimes becoming their offices, and they have as much life as a sign that graces their office doors. Their relationships to the human and the Holy are depersonalized, dehumanized. By denying their bodies, repressed persons cut themselves off from a source of truth that provides direct, immediate, and pure contact with the world. We must all learn to listen to the messages our bodies send us concerning feelings of depression, of anger, and, especially, of a sexual nature, for these messages tell us who we are and where we are in the world in relation to other people. We human persons make each other be. Those of us who deny knowledge of any of our feelings also deny other persons. We soon find ourselves alone in an unhealthy solitude. In therapy, we would hope to achieve instead a healthy loneliness, that yearning for others that can restore the interpersonal. But we cannot feel this loneliness if we deny our bodies.

Repressed persons live in a world of ideas and abstractions; they therefore live inauthentic lives. When greeted warmly, they respond abstractly. Their conversation stays in the realm of the theoretical because they fear the personal, the real. Repressed persons live in a sad, cold, and sterile world, a world full of thoughts about feelings. Such a world is very depressing; so repressed persons are often also depressed persons whose world is safe, distant, and detached.

The world of work offers a hiding place, a safe haven, into which we human persons can retreat when we are confused by messages from our bodies, when we do not want to deal with the feelings of which our bodies make us aware. But for the repressed person, work is more than a safe haven; it is a prison. Interpersonal intimacy so threatens repressed persons that they must retreat into functionalism. Often they become workaholics. They are unable to take the risk that the psalmist speaks of because they distrust their feelings. They find that they cannot trust others unless they meet them on the narrow ground of the functional world, unless they meet them in terms of their stations, their offices, their functions. In the functional world, repressed persons are able to organize, manage, and control their feelings and the messages from the world that are revealed through feelings. Yet these messages are filtered through such a private code that other persons are unable to speak the repressed person's language. This possibility is especially undesirable for repressed religious professionals who live the shared life of community. As their repression requires them to become more and more isolated, they may find themselves drifting toward a technically specialized world of secular professionals and becoming more and more uncomfortable in community. Their ministries will begin to define their vocation. They will cease being religious and become lay professionals.

Repressed persons who give the impression of being intimate are usually being duplicitous. Repressed persons never respect other persons; they merely consider them as objects to be exploited. When repressed persons try to become intimate, they become unconsciously exploitive. Ironically, the world inhabited by repressed persons is in this way similar to that of sexually promiscuous persons although it is this latter world of feelings and body that the repressed person is often trying to avoid and escape. Repressed persons and sexually promiscuous persons are both idolators caught in a world of pursuing people as objects and doing so with a kind of negative, or reverse, reverential attitude, an attitude that literally *makes* them diminish rather than respect others.

The even greater irony is that interpersonally the lives of sexually promiscuous persons offer much more promise of conversion to the Holy than do those of repressed persons. Repressed persons are often unconsciously aware of their avoidance of the Holy. Perhaps this point can be made more clearly if we examine what the repressed person strives so hard to deny.

## INTIMACY AND AUTHENTIC GENITAL ENCOUNTER

Authentic or personal genital encounters between men and women are characterized by an interpersonal holiness. During such an encounter, each person first discovers that the other person's body reacts differently from his or her own. Men find that they cannot rush the situation, that they must wait until the woman has had time to prepare to receive and to respond to their advances. Women find that they need the opportunity to await and to dwell with the other person. Both must be patient or both will be dissatisfied. Neither will experience intimacy if the relationship is mutually exploitive.

During an authentic, intimate sexual encounter, the man and woman next experience a moment of excitement when they get lost in each other, when their bodies surrender to each other. This moment is followed by a moment of quiet, of peace, described by one of my clients as a moment of "satisfied sadness." Although it is glossed over in research data, this experience of satisfied sadness is a crucial moment, for during this moment of being alone and yet with another person we discover that we have gone beyond ourselves. Even during the most active encounter, people experience this moment of gentleness and peace. Both promiscuous and committed couples have reported feeling one with themselves and one with each other, especially during this moment of satisfied sadness that follows the encounter.

In that moment we discover experientially that we have been called out of the depths of our solitude to be completed and complemented by the other person. We discover that in the midst of our act of encounter the distance between ourselves and the other person evaporates, that we and the other experience that moment Dietrich von Hildebrand refers to as a moment of mutual self-donation.[4] We are sad about having lost what has been given; during an authentic genital encounter, that gift is a gift of self. The solitude that we are recedes into the background, and true communion with another is affirmed.

Regardless of the intensity of the union, four characteristics are common to all such encounters. First, we experience sexual self-clarification. Sex is a concrete act whereby individual differences are incarnated in a personal style. During an authentic genital encounter, we learn what our aggressiveness or our tenderness evokes in others. We learn how we are with someone. We also discover the physical and psychological flaws of the other. For example, we discover how inextricably the person may be locked into certain patterns of behavior and modes of thought. Second, we feel commitment and responsibility. Because pregnancy is the potential result of such genital encounters, commitment and responsibility are built into the act itself. Illicit lovers experience great anxiety for this reason. Third, we are aware of surrender and loneliness. In the moment of ecstasy, we lose ourselves and leave the whole world behind. Depression follows the ecstasy, a depression characterized by loneliness. The encounter has affirmed that we are oriented toward others, that others exist to complement and complete us. But to give of ourselves we must lose ourselves, just as in every

4. Dietrich von Hildebrand, *Man and Woman* (Chicago: Franciscan Herald Press, 1966).

act of creation there is a dying. Fourth, we desire eternity. When we have had an authentic encounter, we wish to maintain the moment of satisfied sadness forever.

Of course, we need not have genital encounters to be in tune with these dimensions of human nature. But we should understand that intimacy as experienced during the genital act reflects the essential structure of intimacy with the Holy as captured in the psalm. Both are characterized by ecstasy, wonder, risk, and surrender. Unfortunately, repressed persons often cannot allow themselves to know these dimensions in thought or in fantasy. A repressed person's refusal to be sexually *aware* has spiritual implications, for when we deny our bodies, our sexual feelings, we displace the Holy and the fourfold structure of intimacy described above.

I do not submit to contemporary notions of sexual freedom. But I would suggest that the sexually promiscuous person has a better opportunity for conversion than the sexually repressed person. But sexually promiscuous persons must learn to reflect on their behavior, in the light of their commitment and of their experience while they are with their sex partners. Such persons should seek to determine just what it is that they are searching for through the sexual act. If they are true to their experiences, they will discover that the Holy is revealed in the reaction and response of another human being to them. They may find that they are participating in an experience that can promote and lead to transcendence, fulfillment, and completion. But they must remember that without love and commitment the genital act is an unkept promise. At the moment of satisfied sadness, genital sex points beyond itself. The call to sexual intimacy is not an end in itself but a means to the Holy, a means that requires fidelity, commitment, and responsibility. Persons who displace love with sex are constantly in search of new bodies to satisfy their drives; they are forced to do so because they are fixated on the immediacy of sex. But their attempts are futile because they displace the Holy; they ask sex to be the Holy instead of a means by which to discover it. Yet interpersonally sexually promiscuous persons are engaged in a search for meaning. They are searching, whereas repressed persons have withdrawn, too fearful to risk any kind of search, even if it might mean finding out who they are in relation to other people.

## INFATUATION AS AN AVENUE TO INTIMACY

How can we promote a return or an awakening to the contemplative attitude of the psalmist? How can we foster our discovery of the meaning and significance of chaste love, that love that is interpersonal intimacy, that is passionate? Surprisingly, we can achieve these goals through infatuation, an experience that is of great psychological and spiritual importance to each of us. During infatuation, we fall in love with love, not in our heads but throughout our whole being. Infatuated persons are able to experience a love whereby they are deeply and wholly touched by another person. I emphasize this experience of infatuation for two very important reasons. First, while working with religious professionals who are repressed, my experience suggests that they have been denied the opportunity to be infatuated. For priests and religious that denial has often come during seminary or novitiate. Second, infatuation is our first interpersonal experience of a charismatic love relationship on the human level, a love relationship that calls us out of ourselves, calls us to be totally and completely available to another person. Ideally, this experience should occur during adolescence or young adulthood, the period when we are most sensitive to the spiritual, nonfunctional values that are immanent to this experience. However, because counseling or spiritual direction offers us an opportunity to become sensitive to such values, we can be guided through this experience later in life.

Infatuation is characterized by surrender, receptivity, ecstatic loss of self, and risk. Our recollections of being infatuated are replete with pathos and humor. One of my clients described a baseball game during which she was pitched to by a young man with whom she was infatuated. He threw the ball; she stood in the way and got a black eye. Now that is being deeply touched by another human being!

When we are infatuated, the very presence of the other person is a spontaneous appeal that calls us up and out of ourselves. The loved one evokes in us a feeling of awe; the loved one is a person who walks in mystery. We glorify every characteristic that the person embodies; the good and the bad become the same and are elevated. Every characteristic is lovingly accepted; flaws are overlooked. The mystery that the person embodies is an unspoken command to follow, to imitate the person's every action, regardless of its significance. The person radiates magic that is contagious. When infatuated, we can be made ecstatic by a smile, a touch, a gesture. One of my clients described having dropped her lunch tray when her novice mistress smiled at her because that smile was meant only for her.

Although when infatuated we overlook the flaws of the loved one, we magnify our own imperfections until a small blemish on our face covers our whole face or a flaw in our personality ruins our whole personality. Yet in the presence of the loved one we feel very unique. We feel united in wonder with the other person even if that person does not share our infatuation. Our involvement with the person is total. The person's wishes and needs prevail whereas ours recede into the background. We serve anything that the person wants and regard what we want as totally unimportant. Yet while feeling totally unimportant, we feel that we can accomplish great feats, that no challenge is beyond our power, regardless of the pain, as long as it serves to enhance the loved one. We seek to share our innermost secrets, thoughts, desires, fears, and worries. Our ultimate desire is to become totally visible, giving of ourselves with no thought of reciprocity. Our primary motivation is to be open so as to express eternal love.

When we reflect upon this experience, is it not similar to a conversion experience? The experience includes all of the elements of the prayer of intimacy; it includes fascination, reverence, risk, and a desire to surrender in willing obedience. Obviously, the infatuation experience is not all positive; one of its negative features is that the loved one is often taken by surprise. The person often has not invited the attention and feels quite embarrassed. His or her attitude may lead to serious and painful complications.

Infatuation can be an important experience for our growth in the spirit. We need to learn more about this experience and the way in which the sacred manifests itself in it if we wish to avoid creating an atmosphere that forces the celibate person to flee into a life of repression or sexualism. We need to discover how moments of infatuation give way to moments of love, to moments of intimacy with others and with God.

Sister Virginia O'Reilly, O.P., Ph.D., is a full-time psychotherapist at the House of Affirmation in Montara, California. A member of the Adrian Dominican Sisters since 1944, Sister O'Reilly received her doctorate in clinical and developmental psychology from the California School of Professional Psychology, San Francisco. She was awarded a Danforth Foundation Graduate Fellowship for Women to support these studies. Sister O'Reilly did her undergraduate studies at Barry College, Miami, Florida, and holds graduate degrees from the Catholic University of America and from Siena Heights College, Adrian, Michigan. She has done additional graduate studies at various colleges and universities throughout the United States. Prior to joining the staff of the House of Affirmation, she was an educator, a guidance counselor, and the founding Director of Studies for the Adrian Dominican Congregation. She has worked as a consultant to the Center for Applied Research in the Apostolate (CARA) and has been active on the Sisters Council Executive Board of the Archdiocese of San Francisco. She is a Fellow of the Society for Values in Higher Education and a member of the California State Psychological Association, the National Association of Women Religious (NAWR), and Network, a religious lobby in Washington, D.C.

# RELATIONSHIPS IN THE MIDDLE YEARS

## Virginia O'Reilly

We midlifers, celibate, ecclesial women and men who have entered our middle years, established our sense of who we are as persons in young adulthood. Yet the role models of service to the Church and its people that claimed our youthful idealism have changed, shifted, and all but disappeared. We have been in transit all our adult lives: we have shifted from Latin to English in the Mass, from Gregorian chant to guitars in music, and from "Father knows best" to dialogue with the Parish Council and the Parent-Teacher Association. The crisis of intimacy that the psychologist Erikson identifies as essential to the gradual deepening and opening of the personality was for us largely a matter of finding that persons responded to our ministry in a direct ratio to whatever peace, personal responsibility for the common good, and ability to face reality that we were able to develop. We found experientially that individuals responded to our message of love in direct proportion to the tenderness and warmth with which we were able to communicate that message. We learned that fidelity, acceptance, and trust of our fellow workers were ways to strengthen our dual commitments to celibacy and to deep love of our neighbor. In a word, without knowing either that these were crises, or that we were going through them, we resolved, according to our fashion, what we can now label the crises of identity and intimacy.

It is often noted that the decades during which we are privileged to live seem to constitute a transitional period between two great cultural epochs: the one, rapidly fading into oblivion, comprised the known, the secure, and the familiar. The new epoch is still too formless for us to see anything except its most general outlines. We know, however, that it promises to be very different. Like Abraham, our whole culture has set out on a journey, not knowing *where* it is going, only with *whom.* The journey is one during which all of the Western cultural forms appear to be in a state of change.

For those of us who at midlife are ecclesial women and men, life is especially poignant. After all our learning, all our experience, may we reasonably hope that the roles and the rules, the dreams and the ideals that have served us well during the first half of our lives will carry over into the second half? We may not so hope. The roles, rules, dreams, and ideals do not and will not serve us, for they cannot. The second half of life must have its own significance.

If we remember that as recently as 1900 the life expectancy of men and women in the United States was forty years, it is easier to understand why it is the present generation of men and women at midlife who must face not only the transition process of the culture, but the creation of new roles for ecclesial women and men. Until the very recent past, there has been a paucity of treatment of the developmental aspects of the second half of life even among psychological theorists. We who are presently at midlife are representatives of the first generation in human history for whom the average life expectancy extends into the seventh decade. The focus of concern in both the remote and recent past has been on youth.

## DEVELOPMENT DURING THE ADULT YEARS

Do interacting physiological, social, and psychological factors make life different for women and men during the adult years? Douglas Kimmel explains:

> . . . in our society there are pervasive and subtle sex-related norms and expectations: also there are considerable physiological differences between men and women. . . . As a result of

the interaction of these factors, men and women differ in their inner experience and in their psychological makeup. At the same time men and women are probably at least as similar as they are different and there is considerable individual variation. In a sense our society has tended to stress and perhaps amplify differences between men and women where another society might stress and amplify the similarities. . . . For example, a well-adjusted man or woman may be high on both "masculine" and "feminine" qualities if both sets of characteristics consist of similar and different personality traits and are not assumed to be *opposite* one another. Similarly, one woman may be less "feminine" than another, but need not be any more "masculine"; and a man may be highly "masculine" while also relatively high (or low) on "feminine" qualities. As long as it is clear that "masculine" is not necessarily the opposite of "feminine," both sets of personality characteristics may involve positive, adaptive and different qualities. . . . We feel that less confusion results if it is kept in mind that men and women are probably as similar as they are different; they share many of the basic human characteristics of humans in our society. . . .[1]

Jung was the first theorist to point out the capacity of mature human persons to reach another level of psychological development, to become androgenous individuals, capable of a new integration of masculine and feminine qualities and of a new freedom for love and service. In order to understand what such a capacity involves, let us reflect for a moment on the Jungian concept of the conscious and the unconscious aspects of the personality. "Jung has pointed out that, while the sex of an individual determines his conscious attitude, the unconscious will be characterized by a contrasexual nature, and will be personified by a person of the opposite sex."[2] For a man, this contrasexual personification is termed the *anima,* which represents the unconscious feminine aspect related to his conscious masculine posture toward reality. The analogous contrasexual personification for a woman is termed the *animus.*

1. Douglas Kimmel, *Adulthood and Aging* (New York: Wiley, 1974), pp. 130-31.
2. Eleanor Bertine, *Human Relationships: In the Family, in Friendship, in Love* (New York: Longmans, Green, 1958), p. xiii.

In *Aion* Jung described the qualities of these unconscious aspects of the personality:

> Through the figure of the father . . . [the animus of the woman] expresses not only conventional opinions but—equally—what might be called "Spirit," philosophical or religious ideas in particular, or rather the attitude resulting from them. Thus the animus is a . . . mediator between the conscious and the unconscious, and the personification of the latter. [For a man] the anima becomes, through integration, the Eros of consciousness, so the animus becomes Logos: and in the same way that the anima gives relationship and relatedness to a man's consciousness, the animus gives to a woman's consciousness a capacity for reflection, deliberation, and self-knowledge.[3]

Eleanor Bertine explains Jung's concepts as follows:

> The masculine mentality is predominantly impersonal, analytical and discriminating. It tends toward investigation and formulation and is likely to cut a man off from the earth and warm human connections. . . . but the woman can . . . give him a sense of rootedness in the earth and of all the color, vitality and magnetic allurement of life without which his mind is cold, solitary and forbidding. . . . The projected anima enables a man to get his feelings and therefore himself into actual life. To the woman . . . the animus may give freedom through the ability to know her goal and to pursue it consciously. It also gives the courage, initiative and perseverance to hold out in spite of opposition.[4]

Between them, the anima and animus represent psychic forces arising from the unconscious and leading, in the one case, to the feeling and emotional side of life, and, in the other, to the intellectual and spiritual side.

During the first half of the life span, establishing one's individuality through what Erikson termed the crisis of identity and developing the ability to relate closely to another person through what he termed the crisis of intimacy seem to require

---

3. Carl G. Jung, *Collected Works,* vol. 6, quoted in Irene Claremont de Castillejo, *Knowing Woman* (New York: Harper and Row, 1973), p. 171.
4. Bertine, pp. 100, 102.

that the individual rely largely on the conscious aspects of the personality. But because the deepest longing of the human person is for wholeness, the other side of the human response to reality will continue to exert a tremendous attraction upon the personality. Relationships between women and men during the first half of the life span are essentially functions of needs, in the sense that it is through relationships that needs, especially the essential psychological needs for completion, are fulfilled.

Probably no one has more clearly delineated the difference between such need-fulfilling relationships and the next level of intimate human interaction than has Maslow, who distinguishes between D-love, or deficiency love, and B-love, or love for the being of another person.[5] Most love relationships involve aspects of both D-love and B-love. Predominant during the first half of life, indeed essential to personality development through relationship during this period, is D-love. Relationships between men and women in particular are characterized by the way in which conscious aspects of the personality are enriched.

The effect upon a man of such an intimate interaction with a woman is to develop within him aspects of his unconscious that give the impression of new life. "When he is with her, powers come alive in him that he did not know he possessed. The fact that she is able to see, to respond to, even almost to worship, the masculine principle, the logos, which he represents to her, may make some latent spark of the hero or wise man glow within him, so that he feels himself to be truly more than he had been without her."[6] A related effect is observable in the woman who is involved in an intimate relationship with a man. "She blossoms in the sunshine of his love, becoming more alive, more fulfilled, and ever more beautiful because of it. And as the rela-

5. A. H. Maslow, *Motivation and Personality* (New York: Harper and Row, 1954).

6. Bertine, p. 125.

tion progresses, the animus may be transformed into the subjective functions of sensibility and creative feeling."[7]

## EMERGENCE OF A NEW CAPACITY FOR RELATIONSHIP

As the personality matures past the crises appropriate to youth and young adulthood, a new capacity for relationship emerges, rooted in the new level of personality integration that becomes available. The task of the second half of life is to integrate into conscious personality that sexually opposite side of our own nature that has remained largely unconscious. This integration enables an individual to achieve a fuller measure of humanity. The effect is that of reducing the differences and emphasizing the similarities between women and men. "For example, women as they age seem to become more tolerant of their own aggressive, egocentric impulse; while men, as they age, seem to become more tolerant of their own nurturant and affiliative impulses."[8] Yet a very shaky sense of who we are may be the psychological result of attempted integration, and, as Gail Sheehy reminds us, "any time our self-image becomes shaky . . . we can expect our capacity for intimacy to be disrupted too."[9]

I submit that, as usually results from the challenge of a crisis, we midlifers are being called to a new level of growth in our personhood and that an important aspect of this growth is the opportunity to reestablish ourselves as *sexuated* individuals. I am using the term *sexuated* here to mean an acceptance of the psychological capacities for that openness to reality that differentially characterizes men and women, males and females.[10]

---

7. Ibid., p. 128.

8. B. L. Neugarten, "Adult Personality: Toward a Psychology of the Life Cycle," in B. L. Neugarten, ed., *Middle Age and Aging: A Reader in Social Psychology* (Chicago: University of Chicago Press, 1968), p. 140.

9. Gail Sheehy, *Passages: Predictable Crises of Adult Life* (New York: E. P. Dutton, 1976), p. 287.

10. Marc Oraison, *Being Together: Our Relationships with Other People* (Garden City, NY: Doubleday Image Books, 1971), p. 108.

Sheehy explains:

> It is only now, in this mysterious passage leading to our second season, that we confront the sexually opposite side of our own nature. It is a strange and frightening side, not yet made fully conscious. . . . no matter what we have been doing, there will be some aspects of ourselves that have been neglected, and now need to find an expression. In the case of the woman that has put achievement first, midlife may be a time to relax that effort and put more of herself into cultivating friendships, being a companion to a man, being more active in her community, letting a spiritual side come into play.
>
> It is virtually impossible to bring the mystery to resolution without a struggle. The intimacy balance will almost surely be upset. Being open to intimacy depends on a strong identity, including a firm sense of our sexual identity. Any time our self-image becomes shaky, as it does during every passage . . . we can expect our capacity for intimacy to be disrupted too. If we are to emerge from the struggle as whole beings, our sexually opposite side must become conscious.
>
> [In the case of a man] at 50 there is a mellowness and a new warmth. The competitiveness that gave so many relationships an abrasive edge in the past is tempered by a greater self-knowledge. If a man has come to terms with his essential aloneness, parents can be forgiven. If his individuality is no longer threatened, he can be more relaxed with his colleagues and enjoy a new kind of fellowship with his former mentors. If he has stopped measuring his worth by job status alone, he can better enjoy whatever part of his work holds the most meaning for him. And if he has allowed the psychologically opposite side free expression, he may find a true friend in a woman.[11]

The crisis that Erikson described by the terms *intimacy versus isolation* has as its task the achievement of a truly intimate relationship. The next important crisis in the personal development of an individual is, in Erikson's terms, *generativity versus stagnation*. Here the task is to achieve a sense of productive accomplishment through one's occupation or as a parent so that one will have done something that will outlive oneself.[12] Barry McLaughlin explains:

---

11. Sheehy, pp. 286-87, 293.

12. Kimmel, pp. 189-90.

> Central to the crisis of generativity, whatever the mode of life of the individual, is the development of the capacity for selfless surrender of one's personality and energies. In married life this surrender is to one's partner. In religious life it is to Christ, and ultimately to all mankind. Development of such a capacity is the central problem of this stage in the growth of a healthy personality. . . . The crisis of generativity relates primarily to the establishment and guidance of future generations. However, Erikson feels that there are some individuals who, because of special and genuine gifts in other directions and for high motives, do not express their generative drive in parenthood but in other forms of altruistic concern and creativity which absorbed their kind of parental responsibility.[13]

I believe that for ecclesial women and men Erikson's concept of generativity is essentially that integration of the individual that makes possible the development of the love that Maslow describes as B-love, that is, love of the being of the other person.

Through the crisis of intimacy, religious persons learn to ground the love they have for others in their love for God and to thereby fulfill their vow of chastity. Through the crisis of intimacy, such persons learn how they as individuals can open themselves, make themselves available and accessible to others. Through the crisis of generativity, religious persons extend their love to all of mankind, especially to those men and women who are entrusted to the religious person through his or her apostolic mission. With these men and women, the religious person "realizes a spiritual parenthood, loving them with the qualities of generosity and self-forgetfulness that characterized Christ's love for humanity."[14]

What we have termed here the crisis of generativity is experienced differently by men and women. The expression, then, of the spiritual parenthood referred to above will be different for ecclesial women than it will be for ecclesial men. The differences

---

13. Barry McLaughlin, *Nature, Grace and Religious Development* (New York: Paulist Press, 1964), p. 86.

14. Ibid., p. 90.

have been characterized by Sheehy: "If the struggle for men at midlife comes down to having to defeat stagnation through generativity, I submit that the comparable task for women is to transcend dependency through self-declaration."[15] Women in our culture typically spend their early adult years in a nurturing role that involves both dependency and the dedication of energy to the task of fostering life and the development of others. In the typical life cycle of a woman, the development of a strong independent identity is submerged in her efforts to assist the identity development of others. Thus the autumn of a woman's life is the period during which her cultivation of a sense of self is most likely to occur. Sheehy states: "It is not through more caregiving that a woman looks for a replacement of purpose in the second half of her life. It is through cultivation of talents left half-finished, permitting ambitions once piggy-backed, becoming assertive in the service of her own convictions."[16]

If a woman at midlife is to continue her personal development, she must seek her own uniqueness, her individual self. For ecclesial women at midlife, then, there is a natural readiness to respond to the invitation issued by Cardinal Suenens: "[Women] religious have the duty and the right to assume their responsibilities not only in those questions which concern them as women but also in all the vital problems of humanity. The woman religious as woman has a vital contribution to make to the Church and the world."[17]

In a recent address, Nadine Foley, O.P., pointed out that our present culture has little tolerance for repression of the person and noted that contemporary religious women reflect these cultural norms, as signs of the times, in a creative way.

---

15. Sheehy, p. 294.

16. Ibid.

17. Cardinal Suenens, *Coresponsibility in the Church,* trans. Frances Martin (New York: Herder and Herder, 1968), p. 177.

In our sisters we find today one of the evident characteristics
of our times, namely the valuing of persons, that has come
about through exploration into the depths of the human
potential. One of the by-products has been a corresponding rejection of institutional forms and structures which are repres-
sive or demeaning of persons. We would be poor observers of
our times if we did not see the realization of personal worth
and the desire for personal growth in our sisters and among
people all around us as forming a climate uniquely receptive to
the redemptive message of the Gospel. We are poor witnesses
to the Gospel today if our own women are not facilitated in the
human growth process, in the continuing conversion to which
we are all called in the Lord. If today we are still impeded by
structures that are overprotective of persons and stultifying to
their growth, we can scarcely hope to speak the Word of the
Lord effectively to our contemporaries. We can scarcely speak
the Gospel promise of liberation if we appear to be, and are,
persons unfree.[18]

## NEW ROLE MODELS FOR ECCLESIAL PERSONS

It seems to me, as I ponder the developmental stages that we
now realize are possible at midlife and later, that we as ecclesial
women and men have new ground to break if we are, as mature
adults, to transmit through the witness of our own lives a sense
of freedom and dignity to our contemporaries. We of this generation have received traditions and role models concerning ecclesial persons and their interactions that were perpetuated by
persons who did not have the opportunity for such mature adult
development. It is therefore possible that our fidelity to such a
tradition may limit our own development as persons. This
possibility has been addressed by Karl Rahner, who speaks of
"the integral relation between the freedom of self-realization
and the capacity for love."[19] If we as ecclesial women and men
are to continue during our second season to manifest that "the

18. Nadine Foley, "And Miles To Go . . .," address to the Leadership
Conference of Women Religious Assembly, St. Paul, Minnesota,
August, 1975, p. 12.

19. Ibid., p. 14.

glory of God is man [and woman] fully alive" (St. Irenaeus), we need to address ourselves to the issue.

I do not have any answers. I offer only a series of questions; each of us must work out our response to the challenge as we struggle with our own generativity crises. Once again the Lord calls us to ponder, "See, I am doing something new!" (Is. 44:19).

How does the new dimension of personhood brought into being by the developmental changes at midlife affect the relationships between ecclesial, celibate women and men?

In what fashion can ecclesial women and men at midlife work together to acquire and to leave to future generations the hard-won knowledge of what it means to be adult and to be mature?

In what way is it possible for ecclesial women and men at midlife to apply in their interactions with each other the relationship between the freedom of self-realization and the capacity for love noted by Rahner?

What we "term emotional maturity is characterized precisely by an aptitude for *sexuated* relationships and the ability to control *sexual* impulses and desires."[20] It is also characterized by a recognition of one's value as a person, as Marc Oraison explains: "The idea of a successful relationship with someone else is based first of all on a notion of 'mutuality'. . . . each of the two . . . by his encounter with that particular other person, has a conviction for a time of his own absolutely individual value as existing. . . . each party feels himself recognized for what he is by the other, and thus able to accept himself in the same way."[21]

Because of the times in which we live, and because we who are now at midlife have as our task the creation of new role models for the interaction between mature ecclesial women and men, it

---

20. Oraison, p. 110.
21. Ibid., p. 92.

is essential that we work together to fulfill this task in a way compatible with "the Gospel of one who came that all may have life and have it more abundantly. . . ."[22] The current master-general of the Domican Order, Rev. Vincent de Couesnongle, O.P., has cited the need for a fearless acceptance of the emerging characteristics of our contemporary world for the exploration of the significance of these characteristics as theophanies.

> We must learn to go beyond what we are capable of seeing with our human eyes. Things are much more than they seem— they are also signs of the times, pathways toward God, the presence of God, expressions of God. We must recognize God's grace at work in the "better world" which is trying to grow. Behind every reality there is an "ultimate truth" which may be difficult to reach but which is always, in some way or other, leading us back to God.[23]

For those of us at midlife, the crisis of generativity involves the struggle to emerge reborn, authentically unique, with an enlarged capacity to love ourselves and to embrace others. This struggle means uncertainty and learning to be real. We bring to the struggle a body and a heart already scarred from other battles. But we bring a certain beauty, too. I think I can best explain the quality of this beauty by quoting *The Velveteen Rabbit*:

> One day the young rabbit asks the Skin Horse, who has been around the nursery quite some time, "What is real? And does it hurt?"
> "Sometimes," said the Skin Horse, for he was always truthful. "When you are *REAL* you don't mind being hurt."
> "Does it happen all at once, like being wound up," he asked, "or bit by bit?"
> "It doesn't happen all at once," said the Skin Horse. "You become. It takes a long time. That's why it doesn't often happen to people who break easily, or have sharp edges, or who have to be carefully kept. Generally, by the time you are

---

22. Foley, p. 14.

23. Vincent de Couesnongle to Dominican Order, January 6, 1975.

*REAL,* most of your hair has been rubbed off, and your eyes drop out and you get loose joints, and very shabby. But these things don't matter at all, because once you are *REAL* you can't be ugly, except to people who don't understand."[24]

---

24. Marjorie Williams, *The Velveteen Rabbit* (New York: Doubleday, 1958), as quoted in Sheehy, p. 249.

Audrey E. Campbell-Wray, M.A., is ancillary therapies director at the House of Affirmation in Montara, California. In this capacity, she directs the art therapy, activities, and spirituality programs. Ms. Campbell-Wray brings to the staff of the House of Affirmation the richness of her Afro-American culture and a varied educational and experiential background. A native New Yorker, she attended Hunter College before completing a tour of duty with the U.S. Navy as a neuropsychiatric technician. She subsequently received an undergraduate degree in fine arts and psychology from Lone Mountain College, San Francisco; a master's degree in theology from St. Johns University, New York; and a master's degree in applied spirituality from the University of San Francisco. In addition to several years of experience in psychiatric clinics, she spent two years as an art therapist with the Veterans Administration and four years as a Catholic high school religion instructor and retreat program coordinator.

# THE BEAUTY OF INTIMATE KNOWING

## Audrey E. Campbell-Wray

Once I walked along the shore on the wet sand making foot-prints, letting the ocean scream like thunder in my head until I turned and let my vision sail straight out to where the ocean dropped off the edge of the earth. And I said, "God, you are magnificent."

Once I watched a baby sleep. He was a tiny little one, and he slept beside my bed in a dresser drawer that my mother had turned into a bassinet because his mother was ill and hospital-ized for a couple of weeks. I would wake early and just gaze at him until he wakened; then I would change him, feed him, burp him, bathe him, and rock him. He was so precious.

Once I had a first love, probably more properly called infatua-tion. I would have a major coronary when he walked by, and I could not stand to see him talking to another girl. I swore twenty of my closest friends to death pact secrecy, telling each one in-dividually that she was the only one I could trust with this infor-mation, knowing by the law of chance and the ways of the street that he would know all in sixty minutes or less.

Once I spent the night at a convent retreat house, and my ears wakened me early in the morning to the astonishing sound of high pitched voices singing or chanting. I thought I was in heaven, and because I had had a spiritual advisor who told me that there would be no surprises in heaven, I was not surprised when I opened my eyes and heaven looked just like the convent room I had gone to sleep in the night before. I was sure that I was in heaven because I heard the voices of angels, and knowing nothing at that point about the Divine Office, I had no other explanation for that sound.

Once I taught a high school student, a brilliant young woman who took the death and dying course I was teaching to learn what to expect if her next suicide attempt succeeded. During an individual session I was trying to convince her of the joys of individual counseling when I mentioned in passing my high opinion of her intellectual brilliance. I was certain that my comment was not news to her, but suddenly her eyes lit up, and I saw her smile for the first time. She was astonished to hear such good things about herself. Afterward everything I said she heard in golden tones.

These incidents do not necessarily represent or constitute intimate relationships. Intimate relationships take much longer to nourish and grow. But these incidents were encounters with the beautiful, contacts with beauty, glimpses at all that is beautiful.

The aesthetic notion of beauty has philosophical roots, dealing with certain notions about form, harmony, unity, and synthesis. This notion also deals with qualities, standards, and comparisons. Moving into the functional realm of aesthetics, the world of the artist, we speak about beauty in terms of inspiration, total expression, purity, and catching the essence of something. Sometimes what is beautiful seems unspeakable, awesome, wholly present to the point of impinging on our senses, of even attacking our senses. We cannot seem to deny the reality of its presence at that moment of awareness. Beauty has brought us into contact with truth.

I choose to deal with the idea of beauty in terms of its relation to truth—truth in the mode of Being: being who we really are, as persons, or a thing's being what it really is. When my mind and senses are flooded because I have made contact with the truth—

with *who a person really is* or with *what a thing really is*—I am thrown into a state of awe because I have caught, perhaps only momentarily, the *essence* of *something* or *someone.* I have experienced the beautiful.

The beautiful: it is the ocean, the baby, the beloved, the voices of angels, the student whose smile I have seen for the first time. It is the colleague whose tears I have seen for the first time and the client whose pain I have heard for the two hundredth time. All are beautiful. Although sometimes confusing and emotionally charged, they are nevertheless a glimpse of what is real and true.

## THE HUMAN EXPERIENCE OF KNOWING

Today we are reflecting on the challenge of intimacy. Since the dictionary definition speaks both of close, personal, and confidential friendship and, surprisingly, of illicit sexual relationship, it occurred to me that there may be shock value attached to the very word. It may carry an aura of illicitness. Therefore, I believe that intimacy must be spoken about very carefully and very clearly.

Our possible momentary glimpses or experiences of beauty, it seems to me, are highly licit invitations to move from the edge of encounter into an experience of knowing, during which we can ground a fleeting flood of wonder by a mindful apprehension of reality in order to consciously affirm the truth we have begun to unfold. The progression often follows these eight steps:

1. I sense that you are somebody.

2. I feel something inside; I feel inspired or repulsed. At this point I might recognize the other person's beauty and move along quickly in this experience of knowing another. Or I might be quite closed to the beauty of the other for any number of reasons related to my personal and cultural history, in which case the process of coming to know the other will crawl or cease until such time as new openness is achieved. In either case,

however, the remaining steps serve to open the mind to knowing another and dynamically lead the open mind to full acceptance and affirmation of the one perceived.

3. Something causes me to look at you. I see you. If I am open to your beauty, perhaps I gaze at you.

4. I require myself to listen to you. I hear you.

5. Because I have heard, I am reminded that I have feelings that relate to you.

6. I am moved now to share something with you. Maybe I will share how I feel about you or thoughts and ideas I have never before shared or some other words or some material thing, or maybe I will just share some physical space: I will allow you to be in the same room without conflict, without attacking you.

7. I have not touched you yet; so now I will reach out and touch you, which is a decision on my part, and I am vulnerable.

8. We must persevere as we proceed through the open and vulnerable stage.

These eight steps nourish intimate relationships. I can say to the other: I am here, and the atmosphere I offer you is alive with caring, in the biblical sense of knowledge being the full acceptance of experienced love.

The time required for and the sometime roller coaster character of the above steps can be a stumbling block. Fears are also a stumbling block, as are ignorance and armaments. Yet these barriers are all very human. We often arm ourselves with weapons to fight against the human experience of intimate knowing, and we rationalize our responses with faulty absolutes and faulty assumptions. We therefore must remember that in every situation:

To be feminine is not necessarily to be more vulnerable.

To be masculine is not necessarily to be less vulnerable.

To be feeling is not necessarily to be antiintellectual.

To be thinking is not necessarily to be perceiving reality.

To have sexual feelings is not necessarily sinful.

To be touched is not necessarily to be equated with seduction.

To be aware or your body is not necessarily to be preoccupied with it.

To be known is not necessarily to be rejected.

To be held is sometimes very necessary.

The human experience of intimate knowing does not necessarily lead to genital sex.

Consider the action in a cowboy movie. If I keep my weapon and open the door, I am ready to shoot down each person who crosses the threshold. If I put down my weapon but do not open the door, the ceasefire offers no hope of lasting peace. If I put down my weapon and open the door:

To be vulnerable is not necessarily to be crushed.

## HUMAN KNOWING AS THE PARADIGM OF INTIMACY WITH GOD: THE SONG OF SONGS EXPERIENCE

At the House of Affirmation we recognize the need to exemplify healthier modes of being and functioning. I recognized immediately that the Song of Songs experience, a celebration of fidelity and love, is a role model for the human experience of intimate knowing. The Song of Songs has been an embarrassment to many biblical scholars and church leaders throughout the ages because of its sensuousness, its reality. It has long been spiritualized to play down its humanness. Are the feelings too raw? Is the language too explicit? Is the scripture just barely licit if one party is Israel and the other party God?

Chorus:      Return, return, O maid of Shulam,
             return, return, that we may gaze on you!

Bridegroom: Why do you gaze on the maid of Shulam
             dancing as though between two rows of dancers?

             How beautiful are your feet in their sandals,
             O prince's daughter!

The curve of your thighs is like the curve of a necklace,
work of a master hand.
Your navel is a bowl well rounded
with no lack of wine,
your belly a heap of wheat
surrounded with lilies.
Your two breasts are two fawns,
twins of a gazelle.
Your neck is an ivory tower.
Your eyes, the pools of Heshbon
by the gate of Bath rabbim.
Your nose, the Tower of Lebanon,
sentinel facing Damascus.
Your head is held high like Carmel,
and its plaits are as dark as purple;
a king is held captive in your tresses.
How beautiful you are, how charming,
my love, my delight!
In stature like the palm tree
its fruit-clusters your breasts.
I will climb the palm tree, I resolved;
I will seize its clusters of dates.
May your breasts be clusters of grapes,
your breath sweet-scented as apples,
your speaking, superlative wine.

Bride:          Wine flowing straight to my Beloved,
as it runs on the lips of those who sleep.
I am my Beloved's,
and his desire is for me.
Come, my Beloved,
let us go to the fields.
We will spend the night in the villages,
and in the morning we will go to the vineyards.
We will see if the vines are budding,
if their blossoms are opening,
if the pomegranate trees are in flower.
Then I shall give you
the gift of my love.
The mandrakes yield their fragrance,
the rarest fruits are at our doors,
the new as well as the old,
I have stored them for you, my Beloved.

                              [Song of Songs 7:1-14]

A person who is bereft of intimate human experiences cannot make the profound leap to intimacy with God. At the House of Affirmation we repeatedly see clients who cannot experience intimacy with God until they begin to remove the inner barriers to intimacy with human persons, which is experienced love.

I am inclined to agree with the position Rev. Roland E. Murphy, O. Carm., takes in his introduction to the Song of Songs in *The Jerome Biblical Commentary* (Englewood Cliffs, NJ: Prentice-Hall, 1968). The evidence tells us that the Song of Songs is a collection of love poems or songs done in dialogue. It is about the experience of two human beings who are celebrating, about a lover and a beloved delighting, running, playing, describing one another, reminiscing, pledging fidelity, searching, finding, embracing. Because these are very human activities, I ask: are such feelings and human experiences too profane, too indecent to be holy, sacred, to stand on their own without being spiritualized?

Suppose that the Song of Songs is not about Israel and God, but is about us and our intimate other. Can we still see it as sacred and holy and as becoming more and more so as we learn to love with freedom and wisdom? Part of that freedom is to remain fully who we really are, and part of that wisdom is to refrain from dumping all of our needs on that intimate other, expecting that intimate other to satisfy them all. The Song of Songs is holy enough to be in our Holy Book and human enough to teach us about God. I quote Fr. Murphy: "Human love in itself is an echo of the divine love to which it is inherently directed" (p. 507).

## THE BEAUTY OF INTIMACY

In conclusion, I would like to tell a story. Once upon a time, a very young person named M. spent a great deal of time in the parish church, often just sitting alone talking to Jesus or just feeling peaceful. M. never felt peaceful at home because there never was peace at home. M. read many books, wrote many stories, composed many poems, and disliked many people. M. was quiet and reserved, very bright, and outwardly quite pleasant. M. entered religious life.

A few years later, M., a dedicated, well-trained, religious professional, meets an older, seasoned colleague named C. C. holds out a hand filled with a willingness to listen, with friendship, with companionship. C. notices that M. does not sleep well, does not look at C. when they talk, does not like many people, has undeveloped talent, and has no joy. C. decides to spend much time with M., to reach out and touch M. C. takes M.'s hand. C. does not know what else to do, but does provide an atmosphere alive with caring. M. experiences that love but may or may not be able to receive and reciprocate it.

We all know C. people and M. people. What are their alternatives in our communities and dioceses? The beauty of intimacy is the beauty of each of us. The beauty of intimacy is that intimacy essentially is our way to touch the truth of God. Typical of humankind, we learn to touch God by touching one another.

Bride:     Let him kiss me with the kisses of his mouth.
Your love is more delightful than wine;
delicate is the fragrance of your perfume;
your name is an oil poured out,
and that is why the maidens love you.
Draw me in your footsteps; let us run.
The King has brought me into his rooms;
you will be our joy and our gladness.
We shall praise your love above wine;
how right it is to love you.

[Song of Songs 1:1-4]